SOCIAL LEGISLATIONS AND CIVIL RIGHTS OF SCHEDULED CASTES IN INDIA

Social Legislations and Civil Rights of Scheduled Castes in India

Dr. MUMTAZ ALI KHAN
Director
Centre for Research and Development of Dalits
Bangalore—560032 (India)

Uppal Publishing House
NEW DELHI — 110002

UPPAL PUBLISHING HOUSE
3, Ansari Road, Daryaganj, New Delhi-110002

First Edition 1993
ISBN 81-85565-26-0

Printed in India

Published by B.S. Uppal for Uppal Publishing House
3, Ansari Road, Daryaganj, New Delhi-110002
Printed at Sainion Printary, Delhi - 110 032.

DEDICATED

TO

Mr. P.S. Krishnan, IAS (Retd.)
Former Secretary, Social Welfare Dept,
Government of India

for his total commitment to the
cause of the Scheduled Castes
and Scheduled Tribes

Preface

The study on 'Evaluation of Effectiveness of Protection of Civil Rights Act' was funded by the Ministry of Welfare, Govt. of India, New Delhi. This study is the first of its kind in India. The Act contemplates periodical surveys to be undertaken to assess the effectiveness of the implementation processes. But somehow even after two decades, no such surveys have been conducted.

The credit should go to Mr. Munivenkatappa, IAS., Jt. Secretary, and Mr. B.N. Srivastav, Director, Ministry of Welfare, Govt. of India for having encouraged the author to undertake not only the study, but also to make a comparative study by taking the four Southern States. The Ministry sanctioned a sum of Rs. 79,000/- for the study to start with. But for this liberal and encouraging offer, it would have been difficult to complete the project. The author remains grateful to Mr. Munivenkatappa and Mr. B.N. Srivastav, besides the Ministry of Welfare as such.

The process of data collection became rather difficult as time passed on. A number of hurdles surfaced. Since the study was conducted in four states having different regional languages, it was found impossible to complete the field work without the support of the local leaders. Since a large number of local youths in particular helped the research team all names cannot be mentioned here. The author remains grateful to them. Further, the respondents at the field level were generally co-operative and helpful. They also deserve sincere thanks and gratitude.

A number of Officers did extend lot of support. Mr. Badu Rao, IPS., Superintendent of Police, Hyderabad, Andhra Pradesh and his colleagues, Mr. Prem Kumar, IAS., Bangalore, Karnataka, deserve special mention.

Dr. T.S. Narayan Rao, Professor of Economics, Hyderabad went out of way to help the research team in many ways. He assumed the role of Regional Director in one sense, to extend all possible support in Andhra Pradesh. The author is deeply indebted to him.

A number of lower rank police officers, lawyers, activists did extend lot of help to the research team. The author extends his gratitude to them.

I am also grateful to my late wife, Mrs. Noor Ayesha, M.A, B Ed., who gave me all inspiration to work for the Dalits, both in the form of service and research. By the time the field work was half through she expired. This resulted in a setback to me. But her spirit guided and encouraged me to complete the work.

I owe my gratitude to all the research staff, particularly the field workers who had to face many problems. Mr. C.N. Mowlana, Mr. B. Balappa and Miss. Noor Amjadi deserve special mention for the help rendered.

Bangalore Dr. MUMTAZ ALI KHAN

Contents

CHAPTER I

Introduction

Nature of the Problem

Indian social structure has its own unique place in the world primarily because of its caste system. Several sociologists and anthropologists have made indepth studies on this Indian Social system. Among the foreign researchers are : Louis Dumont, Stephen Fuchs, Robert Hardgrave, Hutton and others. The most important Indian contributors are : G.S. Ghurye, Dr. B.R. Ambedkar, Mahatma Gandhi, M.N. Srinivas and others. These authors have traced the origin, development and problems of the Indian caste system.

What is most striking in all these studies is the dehumanized conditions of the Scheduled Castes, popularly known as Harijans. The very people who speak so high of the Hindu religious philosophy and its greatness have done very little to protect the interest of the Scheduled castes who suffer from the stigma of social discrimination and its worst form of untouchability. This strange contradiction that is noticed in the Hindu social system is unparallel in the social history of any part of the world and at any given point of the time.

Though attempts were made sporadically in some parts of the country before independence to mitigate the problems of the Scheduled castes, not much visible results were seen in the Hindu social order. Dr. B.R. Ambedkar became the committed champion of the cause of the Scheduled castes. It is true that Gandhiji too had raised his voice. But Dr. Ambedkar overshadowed Gandhiji on this particular issue.

Anyway, because of the sustained efforts of Dr. Ambedkar and Gandhiji, there were visible signs of change in the attitudes of the Constitution makers. When the Indian Constitution was finally drafted, there was a clear mention of the problem of the practice of untouchability. Art. 17 of the Constitution bars the practice of untouchability in any of its forms. Its practice would result in punishment. In order to give effect to the constitutional safeguard in the form of Fundamental Right, the Government of India got the Untouchability Offences Act of 1955 enacted by the Parliament.

This law, no doubt, superseded a number of regional laws that had been enacted in the pre-independence States of India. The new law became uniformly applicable to all States excepting the State of Jammu and Kashmir. This law suffered from many deficiencies and handicaps. The very word 'untouchability' was neither defined nor explained anywhere. Punishment suggested was very light. Cases were compoundable and non-cognizable. Areas of coverage were limited and left unexplained too. In short, this law was teethless and had very little impact.

It was later found desirable to bring out a new law with better provisions to ensure dignity and status of the Scheduled castes, not only as Hindus but also as human beings. The Parliament Committee appointed for this purpose submitted its report after ascertaining the views of people belonging to several groups, intellectuals, social scientists and other special groups and individuals were also met by this Committee. This report was accepted by the Government of India and a new law called 'Protection of Civil Rights Act' was enacted by the Parliament in 1976 and with this the structure of the former law, namely Untouchability Offences Act of 1955, was radically altered.

The new Law popularly known as PCR Act has a number of improved and effective provisions. The Law makers were no doubt influenced by the Civil Rights movement of the Blacks in America. The Black Panther Movement had brought out radical changes in the social structure and attitudes of people in America. So, it was expected that this new law would usher in a new social order in India.

The amended law contains the following features :

1. The enlarged scope of the Act ;
2. Severe punishment for violation of the law ;
3. Non-compoundable offences ;
4. Cognizable offences and summary trial ;
5. Provision for collective fine.

Rules were framed in 1977 prescribing the procedure for conducting an inquiry as required under sub-section (1) of Section 10-A.

What is more significant is that section 15-A imposes legal obligation on the State Governments that to undertake effective measures necessary for ensuring that the rights arising from the abolition of 'Untouchability' are made available to and are availed of by the persons subjected to any disability arising out of 'Untouchability'. Some of the contemplated measures are :

1. Provision of adequate facilities including legal aid to the persons subjected to any disability arising out of untouchability.

2. The appointment of officers for initiating or exercising supervision over prosecutions for the contravention of provisions of the Act.
3. The setting up of special courts for the trial of offences under this Act ;
4. The setting up of committees at such appropriate levels as the State Government may think fit to assist the State Government in formulating or implementing such measures ;
5. Periodic survey of the working of the provisions of the Act with a view to suggesting measures for better implementation of the Act.
6. Identification of the areas where persons are under any disability arising out of 'Untouchability' and adoption of such measures as would ensure the removal of such disability from such areas.

As new social order based on social justice and social harmony is expected. The State administration including Police and judiciary is also expected to gear up to meet the desired changes.

On the other hand, there is a new social movement launched by various Dalit organizations to assert their constitutional and legal rights. Dr. B.R. Ambedkar's charisma has inspired millions of Scheduled castes. A new leadership is emerging. Educational facilities have awakened the Scheduled caste youths. Political reservation has also done its job fairy and satis factorily. These new forces have emboldened the Scheduled caste youths in particular.

This changing social scene is very significant because the new challenges will not remain mute spectators when social discrimination is practised. Atrocities will be resisted. At the same time, the caste-Hindus will not yield to the threats of law and the Dalits so easily. What they have achieved and retained cannot be given up so soon and so gracefully.

The result is a conflict between the two groups, namely believers in human indignities and inequalities and the challengers who believe in human dignity and equality. On one hand, the PCR Act which has a social mission is looked at from different angles by different social groups. To the caste Hindus it is an unwanted weapon that the Government has made to destroy their traditional hold and status. But to the Scheduled caste it is a desirable instrument to effect a break-through and come out of the controls and threats of the caste-Hindus.

Another social phenomenon is that the Brahmins who are said to be the original practitioners of social distance and social inequalities have now reconciled by and large and are prepared to support the implementation of the Law. Another point is that for various reasons they have generally migrated from the rural to urban areas. Then it is whether the non-Brahmins are against the implementation of the law. Even here, the Backward castes among the Hindus are generally for elimination of social injustices. Then why do non-Brahmin upper caste people remain in the field ? It is generally believed that it is still up against the Scheduled castes. It could partly be due to the fact that they are the masters of the Castes in economic sector. Besides this, with the disappearance of the Brahmins in the rural areas, centre of authority over religious affairs is transferred to the non-Brahmin upper castes.

Thus implementation of the PCR Act has to be viewed in the context of social change and social conflict. The implementation authorities are also a part and parcel of this social system. And therefore, their role is moulded by the social philosophy and attitudes they have inculcated.

CIVIL RIGHTS ENFORCEMENT CELL

Structure

One of the major measures undertaken by the State Governments at the instance of Government of India was to establish a separate body to be in overall charge of implementation of the various provisions of the Act. This body is designated differently in several States. The various names given are Civil Rights Enforcement Cell (Karnataka), Protection of Civil Rights Unit (Tamil Nadu), Protection of Civil Rights Cell (Andhra Pradesh) and Police Squad (Kerala).

In Karnataka the CRE Cell is located at Bangalore and there are four regional cells too. Currently the cell is headed by an Inspector General of Police. To start with one Superintendent of Police was in-charge. From time to time the post was upgraded. There is one Superintendent of Police attached to the Cell. There are few lower grade officers also.

In Tamil Nadu, the PCR Act is being basically enforced by jurisdictional Police Stations. The PCR Unit is headed by one Deputy Inspector General of Police assisted by two Superintendents of Police and other lower grade officers. One speciality is that it has one Sociologist and one Economist.

In Andhra Pradesh the PCR Cell is a part of the C.I.D. It is headed at the State level by a Superintendent of Police who is directly under the control of the Inspector General of Police, C.I.D. The S.P. is assisted by two Dy. S.Ps and others.

In Kerala, there is a special cell at the Police Headquarters headed by a Deputy Inspector General of Police, PCR. Earlier it was headed by a Superintendent of Police. There are two special squads in Kasargod and Palghat districts. Each squad is headed by a Police Inspector and other lower grade officers.

Functions

The main functions of these enforcement bodies centre round the rights given to the Scheduled castes in matters relating to economic schemes, social guarantees, religious equalities, service reservations, etc.

Though three decades are over since the Principal Act was put into force and one decade is over since the major amendments were effected in 1976, there are hardly any significant studies to assess the effectiveness of the Law. Social legislation *per se* is not a sure bet to remove the traditionally deep-rooted attitudes and values. Much depends upon how the law is put into force, how the oppresser and the oppressed are educated, how the Police behaves, how far the judiciary is competent to deal with this special type of social problems. It is also important to find out how effective is the Police- squad or Civil Rights Enforcements Cell.

It is in this context that there is an imperative need to undertake a comprehensive research study to assess the working of PCR Act in different States since the socio-cultural background of the people differs and this variation could also be an imported factor, either in helping or retarding the process of the legislation.

Broad Objectives

1. To find out the awareness of the legal provisions and the measures of the State Government among the people.
2. To examine the working of the various legal provisions contained in the Act.
3. To find out the bottle necks in the successful implementation of the Act.
4. To offer suggestions to the State to ensure speedy removal of the disabilities of the Scheduled Castes arising out of untouchability.
5. To make a comparative study of the position to the four Southern States.

Specific Questions to be Raised in the Study are

1. What steps have been taken by the State to create awareness of the legal provisions among different social groups having conflicting interest ?

2. What are the problems faced by the victims at the time of registration of complaints in the Police Stations ?

3. What are consequences of lodging complaint with the Police ?

4. How does the Police behave at the time of registration of complaints and what are their problems in reality in booking cases ?

5. What are the facilities provided by the State Government including legal aid to the victims and are these facilities effective and adequate ?

6. Have the State Governments appointed various officers for initiating or exercising supervision over the prosecution for the contravention of the law and how effective are these officers and what are the factors responsible for the variation, if any, in their performance ?

7. What are the various committees set up by State Governments and how do they assist the State Governments ?

8. What are the problems faced by the Police in investigation and prosecution ?

9 What are the problems of the judiciary in disposing of the cases speedily ? What could be the remedial measures ?

10. Are the special Courts set up ? How do they function ? What are their problems ?

11. Are cases being tried summarily ? If not, what are the reasons ?

12. Is there any need for mobile Courts and if so, how should it be structure and what should be its functions and *modus operandi* ?

13. How is the concept of "Collective fine" understood by the concerned people and how far is this being practised ?

14. How are the Police-Squads/Civil Rights Enforcement Cells structured ? How are they functioning ? What are their problems and how to make them more effective ?

15. What are the various types of offences booked, how are the cases disposed of and what is the rate of disposal ?

16. What is the role of voluntary organizations among the Scheduled Castes in creating awareness among the people and how far do they help in booking cases, producing witnesses and pressuring the Police to act ?

Another important question that needs to be probed into relates to the status of the cases booked under the PCR Act. Table 1.1 deals with the cases during 1985 and Table 1.2 has particulars for the year 1986.

It is seen that there is an extremely negligible number of cases ending in conviction as against cases ending in acquittal. Further a large number of cases are pending both with the Police and the Courts.

This issue, therefore, assumes great significance. What are the reasons for this ? How people react to this situation ? In fact, this issue becomes the crux of the problem.

RESEARCH DESIGN

Area Sampling : It was planned to conduct the study in four southern states, namely ; Karnataka, Tamil Nadu, Andhra Pradesh and Kerala. It was felt later on that Kerala should be left out since the practice of untouchability is not at all a problem there. There was another opinion that it would still be meaningful if Kerala is included and then find out why Kerala is different from other states. Hence Kerala is also included.

TABLE 1.1

Status of PCR cases in the Southern States during 1985

States	*Brought forward with*		*No. of cases registered during the year*	*No. of cases closed by the police*	*No. of cases challenged in courts*	*Cases ending in conviction*	*Cases ending in acquittal*	*No. of cases pending*	
	Police	*Court*						*with police*	*with court*
Karnataka	679	1770	659	98	506	4	160	734	2112
Tamil Nadu	113	1112	1280	338	944	50	982	111	1024
Andhra Pradesh	213	478	237	61	162	7	25	227	608
Kerala	3	57	27	4	24	—	30	2	50
Total	1008	3417	2203	501	1636	61	1197	1074	3794

Source : Report of the working group on Development of Scheduled Castes during 8th Five Year Plan (1990-95)

TABLE 1.2

Status of PCR cases in Southern States during 1986

States	*Brought forward with*		*No. of cases registered during the year*	*No. of cases closed by the police*	*No. of cases challenged in courts*	*Cases ending in conviction*	*Cases ending in acquittal*	*No. of cases pending*	
	Police	*Court*						*with Police*	*with Court*
Karnataka	153	382	664	58	49	3	34	710	394
Tamil Nadu	111	1024	1228	434	805	59	781	100	989
Andhra Pradesh	227	608	186	70	253	20	188	90	653
Kerala	2	50	32	5	22	3	17	7	52
Total	493	2084	2110	567	329	85	1020	907	2088

Source : As in the previous table.

The research team visited the Headquarters of these States and collected preliminary information about the districts which needed to be included. Two districts from each State were taken. From each State it was originally planned to take 10 villages. But it was found out later on that instead of taking ten villages from Kerala, only five could be taken and 5 more villages were taken from Karnataka. It was also found desirable to have more areas from Karnataka for convenience purpose. Table 1.3 relates to sample area.

TABLE 1.3

Sampling of districts and villages

Areas *States*	*Districts*	*Total No. of villages from each State*
Karnataka	Bangalore and Tumkur	15
Tamil Nadu	Arcot and Dharmapuri	10
Andhra Pradesh	Mahaboobnagar and Warrangal	10
Kerala	Kasargod and Trivandrum	5
Total		40

POPULATION

When the project proposal was submitted it was planned to take 900 respondents covering different categories. Bt at the time of finalising the categories after preliminary exercises and visits to the various areas it was felt desirable to have some changes. The revised schedule of respondents is presented in Table 1.4.

The various categories of respondents are: Scheduled Castes, non-Scheduled Castes, Activists, Police and Miscellaneous category. The last category includes a few judges, public

TABLE 1.4

Distribution of Respondents by Category

Category States	*S. Caste*	*Non-S. Caste*	*Activists*	*Police*	*Miscellaneous*	*Total*
Karnataka	150	75	110	50	30	415
Tamil Nadu	100	50	45	25	15	235
Andhra Pradesh	100	50	45	25	15	235
Kerala	50	25	40	20	10	145
Total	400	200	240	120	70	1030

prosecutors and lawyers. The problems faced in collecting information from this category of respondents are narrated separately under "Limitations" and "Difficulties" at the end of this Chapter.

The Scheduled caste respondents are from the concerned villages. They are both general and some actual victims of the harassment by the caste Hindus. In all 400 Scheduled Caste respondents are taken. Karnataka accounts for the maximum and Kerala for the minimum. Non-Scheduled Castes respondents are 200 in all. Even here and as else where, Karnataka tops the number and Kerala had the least. These non-Scheduled castes are taken from the Brahmins, Non-Brahmin, upper castes and Backward castes.

The next category of 240 belongs to the activists. These activists are mostly Scheduled Castes, besides some non-Scheduled Castes. They are all generally members of the various Scheduled caste organizations. Of course, some do not belong to any formalised organizations. These are the persons with lot of commitment and experience. Their inclusion in the sample gave a lot of benefit since these activists are not under the thumb of the caste-Hindus.

Policy play a vital role in the process of implementation. Hence 120 Police respondents were included. These Police respondents are right from Police constables to the rank of Director General of Police. But the situation varies from State to State. Wherever the DGPs were available and co-operative, they were included in the sample simple since they had experience and were independent. They could express their opinion freely and frankly.

A further break-up of the Police respondents is presented in Table 1.4(a). This includes Scheduled castes, Non-Scheduled castes, Muslims and Christians.

TABLE 1.4a

Distribution of Police Respondents by Social Groups

States	*S. Castes*	*Non-S. Caste Hindus*	*Muslims*	*Christians*	*Total*
Karnataka	20	22	5	3	50
Tamil Nadu	8	9	5	3	25
Andhra Pradesh	8	9	5	3	25
Kerala	4	6	4	6	20
Total	40	46	19	15	120

The last category of 70 respondents consists of 40 lawyers and 30 judges and public prosecutors. Their inclusion was helpful to assess the situation relating to the nature of disposal of the cases brought up under the PCR Act.

Background of the Respondents

1. *Sex* : Though originally it was not planned to go by sex ratio among the correspondents, it was finally found that wherever women respondents were available in a random process of selecting the respondents, some women were inevitable. There was no reason to exclude them when they were inevitable in a usual process of selection.

Out of a total sample of 1030 respondents of all categories, 885 were males and 145 females. It means that about 14% are female respondents as seen in Table 1.5. Kerala top the States. These women respondents belong to several categories. But a vast majority of them are housewives. There are ten Police constables and 20 employees in other services. About 30 are manual labourers. The rest are all housewives.

TABLE 1.5

Distribution of Respondents by sex

States	*Sex*		
	Male	*Female*	*Total*
Karnataka	375	40	415
Tamil Nadu	200	35	235
Andhra Pradesh	210	25	235
Kerala	100	45	145
Total	885	145	1030

(2) *Occupation* : The respondents belonged to various occupational groups ranging from the lowest status yielding

occupations to the elite group and enjoying a very high status. The related distribution is indicated in Table 1.6.

The maximum number of 445 comes from the Government sector which consists of employees in public sector such as banks, factories, educational institutions, both Central and State Government offices, Public prosecutors, judges, etc.

Next to this category of occupation is the manual labour. This includes mostly farm labourers and then industrial labourers. This sector accounts for 335 in all. Private sector has 130 respondents. They are lawyers and employees in private industries. Businessmen numbering 120 belong to mostly petty business and some other type of activities.

(3) *Education* : It is seen from Table 1.7 that a vast majority of the respondents are educated. Those who have had college education account for the largest number. Then come those who had high school education and primary education in the same order. Illiterates account for 32.6%. It is seen that as expected, none of the respondents is an illiterate in Kerala.

Tools for Data Collection

Four tools were employed to collect data from the respondents. This depended upon the category of respondents. These are : Interview Schedule, questionnaire, group discussion and case-study. These are all the primary sources of information. The secondary source of information consists of published and unpublished documents containing relevant information.

Interview schedule method was adopted primarily to collect information from the illiterate respondents, activists, police, lawyers and judges. Questionnaire method was used in limited cases since this method did not help the research team. Most of the respondents did not fill up and send questionnaires mailed to them or handed over to them. One reason for this

TABLE 1.6

Distribution of Respondents by Occupation

States	*Occupation Manual Labour*	*Business*	*Private Section*	*Govt. Section*	*Total*
Karnataka	130	30	40	215	415
Tamil Nadu	90	25	30	90	235
Andhra Pradesh	100	20	35	80	235
Kerala	15	45	25	60	145
Total	335	120	135	445	1030

TABLE 1.7

Distribution of Respondents by Education

Literacy States	*Illiterates*	*Primary Std.*	*High School*	*College*	*Total*
Karnataka	165	50	70	130	415
Tamil Nadu	75	35	45	80	235
Andhra Pradesh	95	30	50	60	235
Kerala	—	20	50	75	145
Total	335	135	215	345	1030

is that they were scared of disclosing their identity as they were mostly officials.

Group-discussion and a few case-studies with knowledgeable persons were extremely useful to get into the insights of the problem.

Analysis and Presentation

The nature of the study warranted only simple statistical analysis wherever needed. Both qualitative and quantitative analysis was done. Data were organized and manually tabulated. The results of this study are presented in six Chapters. Chapter I relates to introduction. Chapter II deals with the Scheduled caste and Non-Scheduled caste respondents. In Chapter III, the role of the Activists is presented. Chapter IV is on the Police. Chapter V has information of the lawyers and judges in matters relating the PCR Act. The last Chapter focusses on broad conclusions and recommendations.

Difficulties

When the project was conceived and it was felt more useful if all the four Southern States are taken up for the study, the actual difficulties and limitations could not be envisaged. It was only when the research team got into business, the problems surfaced and thence certain modifications were inevitable, taking care to see that the objectives of the study are not lost sight of.

The first difficulty was encountered when the Scheduled Caste respondents and their leaders did not show any interest. On the other hand they displayed lot of apathy. The activists were also indifferent. Their main reason was that such surveys and enquiries would not help them. The Government is not interested. Reports are in abundance. "Should the Government need a survey report to know what is happening to us every day ? What happened in Karnataka, Tamil Nadu and

Andhra Pradesh ? It is obvious that the caste-Hindu dominated Government will not do anything for us. Our political leaders are *chamchas*. They are least interested in us. What researchers can do ?"

It took considerable time to convince these people and then enlist their support. It should be admitted that no research can be done if the respondents are cool or angry. The background of the Project Director and his self-less and dedicated service to the down-trodden finally convinced the Scheduled Caste respondents.

Then comes the question of the non-Scheduled Caste respondents. The Brahmins had no reservations. So too were the Backward castes. But the non-Brahmin upper castes were generally tough. They refused to meet the research team. 'Why do you want to provoke the Scheduled castes and encourage them to raise against us. Do you want to report against us ? Why should we waste our time ? Their tough attitude discouraged the research team. It took considerable time to get the non-Scheduled Caste respondents. In fact, some of the interview schedules had to be cancelled because after giving some information they refused.

Police respondents were suspicious of the research team. Some of them at the lower level felt that the report would go against them. Their knowledge would be exposed. They would be transferred. The caste-Hindus would create problems to them. These were some of their apprehensions. Some of them wanted permission letter for the study. They warned the research team about the possibilities of some caste-Hindus misbehaving with them.

In Andhra Pradesh Naxalites created problems to the field investigators. They suspected the investigators. They were asked to answer many questions and establish their bonafides. Finally a copy of the sanction of the research project by the

Government of India and the Project Director's letter authorising field work and the fact that the field investigators were from Karnataka relieved them. Field investigators later on confessed that they had their own fears about their safety.

Judges would just refuse to have any dialogue. They would think that they are not supposed to entertain any discussion about the judicial matters. It was a great problem to get them. Finally a few retired judges had also to be approached. Another problem was that they would not allow long discussions and also filling up of the interview schedule in their presence. Hence the Project Director had to remember their answers and note them later on after leaving the place.

Another difficulty was that the Police, Lawyers and judges were generally not willing to furnish their names and caste groups. Some of them insisted that they should not be quoted. In fact, some were particular that even their places should not be disclosed as this might enable the higher-ups to find out their actual identity.

Language was another problem. The research team originally consisted of only personnel from Karnataka. The staff did not have adequate knowledge of Telugu and Tamil. They could struggle to manage. But they could not understand Malayalam. Therefore the Project Director had to enlist the support of the locally available assistants whose services could be had after convincing the educated and good natured people.

Another problem was about getting statistical information from the concerned officers. In some cases the information was not readily available and in some cases the particulars were not not systematically maintained. Lots of correspondence had to take place. It was only the Director of SC/ST, Government of India based at Bangalore, who helped in the matter.

Limitations

So far as the major limitations of the present study are concerned, it should be admitted that each State has its own pattern, procedures and policies. Drawing definite and unassailable conclusions and making uniform recommendations in the given situation would not be so easy. State-wise indepth study would be more meaningful and effective.

The situation is altogether different in Kerala. Because of the impact of communism, social mobility and educational advancement and also because of the influence of Sri Narayan Guru, a great saint and social reformer, Kerala presents a different scene. Field work in Kerala was therefore, very much restricted compared to other States.

Opinion of the judges in particular is extremely marginal since, as already pointed out, they were not willing to enter into any dialogue on the issue. Hence whatever information is presented in the study is a fraction of what was earlier desired.

Then in terms of selection of respondents and the sample areas, some significant modifications became inevitable when compared to what was designed earlier. This limitation was unavoidable. However, the overall objectives of the study are not in any way affected.

CHAPTER II

Scheduled Castes and PCR Act

The Protection of Civil Rights Act, is no doubt, for ensuring certain basic human rights to the Scheduld Caste people who become victims at the hands of the caste Hindus. One possible question that would arise is whether the Scheduld Caste people are familiar with the Law and the enforcement authorities. What are their perceptions ? What weaknesses they find in the operational system ? Do they have any suggestions to offer ?

Similarly, the non-Scheduled Caste people, particularly the Caste-Hindus, have also their perceptions, opinions and suggestions regarding effective implementation of the PCR Act. Therefore, their views also become very relevant to the present study.

Thus, both the Scheduled Caste and Non-Scheduled Caste respondents should be heard to get some insights into the problem. This is dealt with in this Chapter. The various social variables included here are :

1. Awareness of the relevant legislations,
2. Sources of awareness,
3. Extent of the knowledge about PCR Act,
4. Period of awareness of CRE cell,
5. Awareness of various measures of the State,
6. Problems while registering complaints,
7. Consequences of lodging complaints,
8. Opinion about the police officers,
9. Reasons for ineffective role of the police,
10. Facilities provided by the State,
11. Problems of securing witnesses, and
12. Suggestions for improvement.

Awareness of Legislations

Awareness of legislations relating to social discrimination and atrocities is an important factor in mitigating the problems. The Scheduled castes are the persons who are the targets of exploitation and social discrimination. The more awareness is found among them, better are the possibilities of relief. Hence, awareness of the three important legislations among them is examined. The relevant data are presented in Table 2.1.

Untouchability Offences Act (UOA) is known in general only to 25% of the total respondents, it means that three-fourth of them have no awareness of this law which has been in existence for the last four decades. Among the different States, it is in Kerala that the majority are aware of this law (60%), while Andhra Pradesh has the lowest percentage of 15, Karnataka and Tamil Nadu are slightly better than Andhra.

There is some meaning if the majority are not aware of Untouchability Offences Act. They should atleast be aware of

TABLE 2.1

Awareness of legislations among the Scheduled Castes

States	*Untouchability offences Act*			
	Aware		*Not Aware*	
	N	*%*	*N*	*%*
1	2	3	4	5
Karnataka N=150	30	20.0	120	80.0
Tamil Nadu N=100	25	25.0	75	75.0
Andhra Pradesh N=100	15	15.0	85	85.0
Kerala N=50	30	60.0	40	40.0
Total	100	25.0	300	75.0

Protection of Civil Rights Act				SC/ST Abolition of Activities Act			
Aware		Not Aware		Aware		Not Aware	
N	%	N	%	N	%	N	%
6	7	8	9	10	11	12	13
35	23.3	115	76.7	10	6.7	140	93.0
30	30.0	70	70.0	12	12.0	88	88.0
10	10.0	90	90.0	10	10.0	90	90.0
34	68.0	16	32.0	15	30.0	35	70.0
109	27.2	291	72.8	47	11.7	353	88.3

the Protection of Civil Rights Act (PCR Act) which is in force today and cases are booked under that. But it is seen from the table that there is not much awareness of this law also. The average percentage of awareness in just 27 which is slightly but insignificantly higher than the awareness of U.O. Act. State-wise position is also distressing excepting in the case of Kerala where it is 68%. Andhra Pradesh accounts for the lowest percentage of 10. Tamil Nadu and Karnataka are much better.

Awareness of SC/ST Abolition of Atrocities Act is the lowest. On an average only 12% are aware of this law which came into force during 1989. Among all the states, Kerala accounts for the highest percentage of :0 whereas the other states present a dismal picture. Karnataka is the worst of the lot.

Sources of Awareness

Since the Scheduled Caste respondents are mostly illiterates and they have low level of awareness of the PCT Act, sources of awareness becomes quite relevant. Table 2.2 has seven sources of awareness. These are newspaper, radio, television, friends, activists, government and social conflicts. Respondents could furnish multiple answers.

In general 92% of the total repondents get information through newspapers. They say that sometimes newspapers report about cases booked under the PCR Act and thus they come to know. While in Tamil Nadu and Andhra Pradesh 100% respondents quote newspapers, a little more than 85% of the respondents of Karnataka and Kerala give this source. What is surprising here is that Kerala comes next to Tamil Nadu and Andhra Pradesh.

Radio is quoted by 67% respondents in general. This is not very effective, according to the respondents Kerala stands first and Karnataka last. So far as T.V. is concerned, Kerala again

TABLE 2.2

Sources of Awareness of P.C.R. Act among the Scheduled Castes

States	*News Paper*		*Radio*	
	N	%	*N*	%
1	2	3	4	5
Karnataka N=35	30	85.7	15	42.9
Tamil Nadu N=30	30	100.0	20	66.7
Andhra Pradesh N=10	10	100.0	8	80.0
Kerala N=34	30	88.2	30	88.2
Total N=109	100	91.7	73	66.9

T.V.		Friends		Activists		Government		Social conflicts	
N	%	N	%	N	%	N	%	N	%
6	7	8	9	10	11	12	13	14	15
25	71.4	20	57.1	30	85.7	15	42.9	35	100.0
25	83.3	25	83.3	25	83.3	15	50.0	20	83.0
8	80.0	87	80.0	7	70.0	15	50.0	10	100.0
30	88.2	20	58.8	20	58.8	20	58.8	20	58.0
88	80.7	73	66.9	82	75.2	55	50.4	90	82.6

Note : Multiple sources were quoted by the respondents

comes first and Karnataka last. Tamil Nadu and Andhra Pradesh come in between.

'Friends' is another source with 67% respondents quoting this. Friends inform the Scheduled Caste people about the law and it is learnt from them that only marginal references are made to the existence of law.

'Activists' form another important source. Seventy five per cent respondents quote them in general. Karnataka stands first and Kerala the last. What is further learnt is that the activists start agitating against the cast-Hindu and in that process tell the people that the PCR Act gives guarantee of certain Civil rights.

'Government' is the least quoted source with just 50%, it means government has not made adequate arrangements to create the awareness of the law among the Scheduled Castes. This is the position in all the four States. Even in Kerala only 58% respondents quote this.

'Social conflicts' form the second best source of information. Whenever conflicts take place, the issue becomes a subject for hot discussion, agitation and tensions. People became curious and in the process they come to know about the law. In general 83% quote this source. While in Karnataka and Andhra Pradesh 100% quote this, Kerala has the lowest percentage. It is possibly because of the social situation which does not witness conflicts in Kerala as seen elsewhere. Even the 59% Keralites give this source as they know what is happening in other states.

Awareness Among Non-Scheduled Castes

Though these legislations are for the benefit of the Scheduled castes, indirectly they also concern the caste-Hindus and other Hindus. Those who are found guilty of violation of the law will be punished and therefore they should also be aware of the legislations. To what extent the Non-Scheduled caste people are aware of the three legislations ? Table 2.3 presents the data.

Untouchability Offences Act is known in general to 20% Non-Scheduled castes. When compared to the awareness among the Scheduled castes, Non-Scheduled castes account for a slightly lower percentage. Among the different States, Kerala tops with 40% and Andhra Pradesh has the lowest percentage. Karnataka is slightly better than Andhra. But Tamil Nadu is closer to Kerala.

PCR Act is known to 19% respondents in general. Even here Scheduled castes stand better. Kerala has the highest percentage of 40%. Tamil Nadu is closer to Kerala. Andhra Pradesh is the worst with just 8%.

Awareness of SC/ST Abolition of Atrocities Act is the least in the series. Just 9% Non-Scheduled caste respondents know this. Among the various States, Kerala stands first with 20% Andhra Pradesh is the worst. Kerala is the progressive State and people are educated. But even in such a State, awareness is not encouraging.

Sources of Awareness

Sources of awareness among the non-Scheduled castes are also in tune with those of the Scheduled castes. Only percentage variations are found. Table 2.4 has relevant information.

It is seen that 'social conflicts' happens to be the best source. Ninety four percent respondents have quoted this in general. State-wise speaking, it is only in Tamil Nadu that 93% respondents have referred to this. In all the other States, there is 100% reference.

'Newspapers' accounts for 82% in general and in Andhra Pradesh and Kerala there is 100% reference to this. Eighty

TABLE 2.3

Awareness of Legislations among the Non-Scheduled Castes

States	*Untouchability Offences Act*			
	Aware		*Not Aware*	
	N	*%*	*N*	*%*
1	2	3	4	5
Karnataka N=75	10	13.3	65	86.7
Tamil Nadu N=50	15	30.0	35	70.0
Andhra Pradesh N=50	5	10.0	45	90.0
Kerala N=25	10	40.0	15	60.0
Total N=200	40	20.0	160	80.0

Protection of Civil Rights Act				*SC/ST Abolition of Actrocities Act*			
Aware		*Not Aware*		*Aware*		*Not Aware*	
N	%	*N*	%	*N*	%	*N*	%
6	7	8	9	10	11	12	13
10	13.3	65	86.7	5	6.7	70	93.3
15	30.0	35	70.0	5	10.0	45	90.0
4	8.0	46	92.0	3	6.0	47	94.0
10	40.0	15	60.0	5	20.0	20	80.0
39	19.5	161	80.5	18	9.0	182	91.1

TABLE 2.4

Sources of Awareness of P.C.R. Act among the Non-Scheduled Castes

States	*News Papers*		*Radio*	
	N	%	*N*	%
1	2	3	4	5
Karnataka N=10	8	80.0	8	80.0
Tamil Nadu N=15	10	66.7	12	80.0
Andhra Pradesh N=4	4	100.0	3	75.0
Kerala N=10	10	100.0	10	100.0
Total (N=39)	32	82.0	33	84.6

T.V.		*Friends*		*Activists*		*Government*		*Social Conflicts*	
N	%	*N*	%	*N*	%	*N*	%	*N*	%
6	7	8	9	10	11	12	13	14	15
8	80.0	6	60.0	8	80.0	6	60.0	10	100.0
12	80.0	8	53.3	7	46.7	7	46.7	14	93.3
3	75.0	3	75.0	3	75.0	2	50.0	4	100.0
10	100.0	—	—	4	40.0	10	100.0	10	100.0
33	84.6	17	43.6	22	56.4	25	64.1	38	97.4

five per cent respondents give radio as well as T.V. as a source. State-wise position is that while in Kerala 100% quote this, Andhra Pradesh has the lowest percentage of 75, Karnataka and Tamil Nadu are slightly better.

'Friends' and 'activists' are quoted by 44% and 56% respondents in general. While none in Kerala quotes this, Andhra Pradesh has the highest percentage with 75%. Karnataka and Tamil Nadu are next to Andhra.

'Government' as a source of information is quoted by 64% respondents in general. While in Kerala 100% respondents mention this, the least is in Tamil Nadu with 47%.

Extent of Knowledge

It is indicated earlier that 109 out of 400 Scheduled caste respondents have heard of PCR Act. But the real issue relates to the extent of knowledge of the Act. This is discussed with reference to the data presented in Table 2.5.

It seen that those who have partial knowledge constitute 69% in general. Among the respondents of Karnataka as high as 83% have partial knowledge and it is 100% in Andhra Pradesh. Kerala has a good performance with 41% respondents saying that they are mostly knowledgeable. While none in Karnataka and Andhra Pradesh have full knowledge, there is a small percentage in Tamil Nadu and Kerala having full knowledge.

The respondents were further put to test in group discussions about their knowledge when they said that they have full knowledge or most of the knowledge or partial knowledge. When tested very carefully, it was found that their knowledge was extremely limited.

Awareness of Measures

The State governments have undertaken certain special measures as required under the law for effective implementation

TABLE 2.5

Extent of Knowledge of P.C.R. Act among the Scheduled Caste Respondents

States	*Fully knowledgeable*		*Mostly knowledgeable*		*Partly knowledgeable*		*Total*	
	N	%	*N*	%	*N*	%	*N*	%
Karnataka	—	—	6	17.1	29	82.9	35	100.0
Tamil Nadu	2	6.7	8	26.7	20	66.6	30	100.0
Andhra Pradesh	—	—	—	—	10	100.0	10	100.0
Kerala	4	11.8	14	41.2	16	47.0	34	100.0
Total	6	5.5	28	25.7	75	68.8	109	100.0

of the law. Some of these measures as known to Scheduled castes as presented in Table 2.6 are : CRE Cell, mobile courts, special courts, summary trials and collective fine. The question now is to what extent the Scheduled caste and Non-Scheduled caste respondents are aware of these measures.

Civil Rights Enforcement Cell is known to just a small number constituting 21% in general. The State wise position is too bad excepting in Kerala where 50% are aware of this. Awareness of mobile courts is still worse. Only 11% respondents are aware of this. Even here Kerala tops with 36% and the rest of the States are far below this percentage.

'Special courts' are not known to a vast majority of 89% respondents in general. It means only 11% are aware. Kerala tops with 38% and the rest do not even touch two figures. 'Summary trial' concept is known only to 7% in general. While none know in Karnataka and Andhra, Kerala accounts for 40% and Tamil Nadu has a very low percentage.

The much talked about 'collective fine' is hardly known to the respondents. It draws blank in three States and it is only in Kerala that a small number constituting 20% is aware of.

Period of Awareness of CRE Cell

The CRE Cell is created for the advantage of the Scheduled caste victims. It could generally be expected that this cell is known to all the Scheduled castes. But table 2.7 is clear that 47% of them happen to know it only during the last year and the rest beyond that period. Even here 36% knew during the last 5 to 10 years as against 16% before this period.

State-wise position is that excepting Kerala where only 20% knew during the last 5 years, the majority of the respondents of other States knew during this period. Further, those who knew during the last 5 to 10 years period are more in number than those who knew it for 10 years and beyond.

TABLE 2.6

Awareness of Certain Measures of the State among the Scheduled Castes

States	*CRE Cell*				*Mobile Courts*			
	Aware		*Not Aware*		*Aware*		*Not Aware*	
	N	*%*	*N*	*%*	*N*	*%*	*N*	*%*
1	2	3	4	5	6	7	8	9
Karnataka N=150	25	16.7	125	83.3	10	6.7	140	93.3
Tamil Nadu N=100	20	20.0	80	80.0	12	12.0	88	88.0
Andhra Pradesh N=190	15	15.0	75	75.0	6	6.0	94	94.0
Kerala N=50	25	50.0	25	50.0	18	36.0	32	64.0
Total N=400	85	21.2	305	76.2	46	11.5	354	85.5

Special Court				Summary Trial				Collective Fine			
Aware		Not Aware		Aware		Not Aware		Aware		Not Aware	
N	%	N	%	N	%	N	%	N	%	N	%
10	11	12	13	14	15	16	17	18	19	20	21
10	6.7	140	93.3	—	—	150	100.0	—	—	150	100.0
8	8.0	92	92.0	10	10.0	90	90.0	—	—	100	100.0
6	6.0	94	94.0	—	—	100	100.0	—	—	100	100.0
19	38.0	31	62.0	20	40.0	30	60.0	10	20.0	40	80.0
43	10.7	357	89.2	30	7.5	370	92.5	10	2.5	390	97.5

TABLE 2.7

Period Since When CRE Cell is Known, According to the Schedule Caste Respondents

States	*10 years ago*		*5—10 years*		*Less than 5 years*		*Total*	
	N	%	*N*	%	*N*	%	*N*	%
Karnataka	2	8.0	8	32.0	15	60.0	25	100.0
Tamil Nadu	4	20.0	6	30.0	10	50.0	20	100.0
Andhra Pradesh	—	—	5	33.3	10	66.7	15	100.0
Kerala	8	32.0	12	48.0	5	20.0	25	100.0
Total	14	16.4	31	36.5	40	47.1	85	100.0

In short, awareness of this important cell is made known to the Scheduled caste respondents by and large during the last 5 years excepting in the case of Kerala.

Awareness of Measures

The various measures of the State are expected to be known to the non-Scheduled Caste people too so that they could avoid violation of the State rules, procedures and so on. In the earlier table the special measures of the State were presented and discussed so far as the Scheduled caste respondents are concerned. In the present Table 2 8, an attempt is made to assess the awareness of this issue among the non-Scheduled Caste respondents.

Civil Rights Enforcement Cell is known to 24% non-Scheduled Caste respondents in general. Thus, a vast majority is not aware. The position among the various States is not uniform. While in Kerala 76% are aware of the Cell, in all the other States, awareness is very poor.

The concept of mobile courts is known only to 15% respondents in general. As seen earlier, even here Kerala tops with 72%, while the other States account for a very low percentage. This is also the position in relation to the special courts. Only 22% respondents in general are aware of this. Kerala tops with 76% and the other States are far behind.

Summary trial is known to a very small percentage. While in Kerala 72% are aware and Tamil Nadu accounts for a small percentage, there is none in Karnataka and Andhra Pradesh being aware of this. The situational analysis with reference to the concept of 'Collective fine' is still worse. Only 4% in general and 32% in Kerala are aware of this. None of the respondents of other States have heard of 'Collective fine'.

In group discussions, a vast majority of the respondents expressed their surprise at the questions. "We have not heard

TABLE 2.8

Awareness of Certain Measures of State among the Non-Scheduled Castes

States	*CRE Cell*				*Mobile Courts*			
	Aware		*Not Aware*		*Aware*		*Not Aware*	
	N	%	*N*	%	*N*	%	*N*	%
1	2	3	4	5	6	7	8	9
Karnataka N=75	10	13.3	65	86.7	4	5.3	71	94.7
Tamil Nadu N=50	12	24.0	38	76.0	6	12.0	44	88.0
Andhra Pradesh N=50	8	16.0	42	84.0	3	6.0	47	94.0
Kerala N=25	19	76.0	6	24.0	18	72.0	7	28.0
Total N=200	49	24.5	151	75.5	31	15.5	169	84.5

Special Courts				Summary Trial				Collective Fine			
Aware		Not Aware		Aware		Not Aware		Aware		Not Aware	
N	%	N	%	N	%	N	%	N	%	N	%
10	11	12	13	14	15	16	17	18	19	20	21
8	10.7	67	89.3	—	—	75	100.0	—	—	75	100.0
10	20.0	40	80.0	6	12.0	44	88.0	—	—	50	100.0
8	16.0	42	84.0	—	—	50	100.0	—	—	50	100.0
19	76.0	6	24.0	18	72.0	7	28.0	8	32.0	17	68.0
45	22.5	155	77.5	24	12.0	176	88.0	8	4.0	192	96 0

of so many issues you are now raising, sir. Nobody has told us about all this". It is further interesting to know that the Backward Castes and non-Brahmin upper Caste respondents have generally no knowledge of this. Only Brahmins have known these, besides a small section of the non-Brahmin upper castes.

Further, literacy level has relevance to awareness. Only those who have had atleast upper primary level of education are aware of all these.

There was also a general dislike for these special measuses among some people. "Why the government wants special treatment to the Scheduled Castes in all spheres of social activities ?", Were the remarks of some.

Period of Awareness of CRE Cell

As seen earlier only 49 out of 200 non-Scheduled caste respondents have heard of CRE cell. Another related issue discussed with them is the period of awareness. In general it is seen from Table 2.9 that 49% have known CRE Cell during the last 5 years even though it came into existence long ago. In Karnataka and Andhra Pradesh all the non-Scheduled caste respondents could know only during this period. The position in Tamil Nadu is Much better. There, 25% knew more than 10 years ago and a little more of them between 5 and 10 years ago. The best position comes from Kerala where 63% came to know more than 10 years ago and 32% during the last 5 to 10 years.

When compared to the position of the Scheduled Caste respondents as seen in the earlier table, non-Scheduled Castes are better in the sense that 31% knew 10 years ago, whereas only 16% knew it during this period. But the overall position is better among the Scheduled Caste respondents rather than non-Scheduled Caste respondents. The main reason for this is that 63% non-Scheduled-Castes respondents of Kerala knew it 10 years ago.

TABLE 2.9

Period Since When CRD Cell is Known According to the Non-Scheduled Caste Respondents

States	*10 years ago*		*5 to 10 years*		*Less than 5 years*		*Total*	
	N	*%*	*N*	*%*	*N*	*%*	*N*	*%*
Karnataka	—	—	—	—	10	100.0	10	100.0
Tamil Nadu	3	25.0	4	33.3	5	41.7	12	100.0
Andhra Pradesh	—	—	—	—	8	100.0	8	100.0
Kerala	12	63.1	6	31.6	1	5	19	100.0
Total	15	30.6	10	20.4	24	49.0	49	100.0

Problems in Registering Complaints

When the Scheduled Caste victims of untouchability or social discrimination go to the Police Station, how are they treated ? Are they heard and their complaints registered ? The reactions of the Scheduled Castes respondents to these questions are contained in Table 2.10.

There was none who could say that he had no problem at all. In varying degrees, respondents could give several problems they face. There are five problems. These are : non-availability of officers, refusal to receive complaints, attempt to effect compromise, threats and rude or indifferent treatment by the Police.

Nearly 19% respondents in general said that whenever they go to the Police Station, concerned officers will not be available. They have to go to the Station situated sometimes far away only to be disappointed. This general view is shared more or less equally by about 20% respondents in the four States.

Fifty per cent respondents said that initially the Policemen would refuse to register the complaints on some grounds. It is only when they press or threaten that they would go to the Dalit organization or higher officers that the Police would accept the complaints. While there was none in Kerala who gave this problem, there are people in substantial number giving this problem in other States. The largest number is in Andhra Pradesh.

The Police is not expected to effect any compromise after the commitment of the offence. But it is generally alleged that they would do so. In the present study 34% respondents in general said that the Police try to effect compromise when the victims go to Police Station with complaints. There are instances where the Police tries to intervene and effect compromise even before the complaint is taken to the Station.

TABLE 2.10

Problems Faced at the Time of Registration of Complaints, According to Scheduled Caste Respondents

States	*Non-availability of Offices*		*Refused*		*Try to compromise*		*Threaten*		*Rude/in different*	
	N	*%*	*N*	*%*	*N*	*%*	*N*	*%*	*N*	*%*
Karnataka N=15	25	16.7	70	46.7	45	30.0	40	26.7	60	40.0
Tamil Nadu N=100	20	20.0	60	60.0	35	35.0	25	25.0	40	40.0
Andhra Pradesh N=100	20	20.0	70	70.0	55	55.0	60	60.0	65	65.0
Kerala N=50	10	20.0	—	—	—	—	8	16.0	10	20.0
Total N=400	75	18.7	200	50.0	135	33.7	133	33.2	175	43.7

There is no such thing in Kerala. No Policeman would even venture to effect compromise. However in the rest of the States this happens, Andhra Pradesh leading in this regard. Respondents were able to give quite a few cases where the Police tried. In some cases they failed and in other case they succeeded. According to the respondents, the Policemen try to do this only after receiving illegal gratification. The caste-Hindus bribe the Police and try to avoid the situation.

Threatening the victims as well as the witnesses is very common to Police culture. In the present case, one-third of the total respondents said so. Andhra Pradesh tops while Kerala has the lowest percentage. When the victims and their supporters go to Police Station, the Policemen would refuse or try to compromise. If this fails, he will have no hesitation to threaten.

Forty four per cent respondents said the Policemen are generally rude or indifferent. Their very presence or voice would be enough to create panic in the minds of the victims. Andhra Pradesh tops with 65%. Kerala accounts for the lowest percentage.

Consequences of Complaints

The traditional social values and attitudes are still so strong that any challenge to the authority of the feudal lords and masters in rural areas is said to be intolerable and full of dire consequences. It is possible that this could be the social situation in the case of the Scheduled Castes in their relationship with the caste-Hindus. This is examined in the present study.

Table 2.11 has seven types of consequences that follow the moment complaints are lodged by the victims. These are : threats by the caste Hindus, grudge, loss of jobs, social boycott, attocities, women in trouble and annoyance of the police. In general 66% of the Scheduled Caste respondents say that they

TABLE 2.11

Consequences of Lodging Complaints with the Police, according to Scheduled Caste Respondents.

States	*Threats by Caste-Hindus*		*Grudge*	
	N	%	*N*	%
1	2	3	4	5
Karnataka N=150	130	86.7	60	40.0
Tamil Nadu N=100	40	40.0	40	40.0
Andhra Pradesh N=100	80	80.0	70	70.0
Kerala N=50	15	30.0	30	60.0
Total N=400	265	66.2	200	50.0

Loss of job		Social boycott		Atrocities		Women in trouble		Annonyance of the Police	
N	%	*N*	%	*N*	%	*N*	%	*N*	%
6	7	8	9	10	11	12	13	14	15
40	26.7	30	20.0	100	66.7	25	16.7	50	33.3
30	30.0	—	—	25	25.0	—	—	25	25.0
30	30.0	40	40.0	60	60.0	30	30.0	50	50.0
—	—	—	—	5	16.7	—	—	—	—
100	25.0	70	17.5	190	47.5	55	13.7	125	31.2

have to face the threats from the Caste-Hindus. It is alleged that some times the threats would be real and the Scheduled Castes cannot bear them.

Among the different States, it is seen that in Karala, issue of threats is most negligible with 30% and Tamil Nadu comes next. But in Karnataka and Andhra Pradesh the situation is alarming.

That the caste-Hindus will keep grudge against the Scheduled Castes was also narrated by 50% respondents in general. When once they have a grudge, they try to harm the Scheduled Caste people in different ways. What is surprising is that Kerala is no exception. But respondents of Kerala said that though sometimes the caste-Hindu have grudge, they are not so harmful. Of course, Andhra Pradesh stands first with 70% respondents. This social phenomenon also prevails in Karnataka and Tamil Nadu, but to a lesser extent.

One significant effect on the Scheduled Castes is that the wrath and grudge of the caste-Hindus would sometimes result in loss of means of livelihood. One-fourth of the respondents in general gave this information. While this is totally absent in Kerala it prevails more or less in equal numbers in other States.

Social boycott is a type of pressure exercised by the caste-Hindus on the helpless Scheduled Castes if they raise their voice againsts the former. Social boycott does real harm to them since it amounts to breaking social order. Presently 17% respondents in general say so, Kerala and Tamil Nadu are free from this. Andhra Pradesh accounts for 40% and Karnataka 20%.

Atrocities in the form of physical violence or some other form of serious damage to the Scheduled Castes was pointed out by 47% respondents in general. Burning the houses or beating up Scheduled Castes or removing the hair on the head and parading them on donkeys are some of the common instances. Forcing the Scheduled Castes consume human excreta or drink urine was also narrated.

State-wise position is that while Kerala has the least number, Karnataka stands first, closely followed by Andhra Pradesh. Tamil Nadu is far better with only 25% respondents mentioning this. In Karnataka, Scheduled Castes youths were forced to consume human excreta in Bendegere village in Belgaum district. In another village they were forced to drink human urine.

Normally women are untouched by the anti-social elements. But there are instances where women have been dishonoured. Nearly 14% respondents in general said that whenever Scheduled Castes men challenged the castes-Hindus, their women have to face the consequences. Kerala and Tamil Nadu seem to be free from this shameful action of men. Andhra Pradesh and Karnataka are still practising this to some extent. Parading women totally nude or semi nude is found here and there.

When complaints are lodged, police feels annoyed because they have to act sooner or later and incur the displeasure and discomfort of the caste-Hindus. Thirty one per cent respondents said that they have to face the annoyance of the people. "Sir, who can provoke the Police and then have peace. It is like provoking the cobra. Police retaliates very badly and we cannot live in peace". The position in Andhra Pradesh seems to be very serious with 50% respondents saying this. Kerala is totally free. Karnataka and Tamil Nadu respondents do say so, but in small numbers.

About Complaints Lodged

Whether complaints lodged by the victims are genuine or cooked up ? It is possible that in the process of taking revenge against their traditional foes, the Scheduled Castes people lodge false complaints in order to take undue advantage of the legal guarantees. It is also possible that the caste-Hindus advance this argument to cover up their misdeeds. Hence it was felt desirable to probe into this aspect.

Table 2.12 furnishes the views of the non-Scheduled Caste respondents. A vast majority of them accounting for 61.5% hold the view that the complaints are real. Of the remaining respondents, 12.5% say that the complaints are always false and 26% hold the view that the complaints are sometimes false.

Speaking with reference to the various States, it is seen that 80% of the respondents of Kerala say so. While the majority of the other States also say so, Karnataka with 53% and Andhra Pradesh with 56% are next to Tamil Nadu.

While there is none in Kerala saying that the complaints are always false, there are some with small percentage holding this view. However, there are a few respondents in all the States saying that the complaints are sometimes false. Karnataka tops with 33.3%, while Kerala has the lowest percentage with 20.

About Police Officers

As pointed out elsewhere, Police is always a crucial and controversial factor in the implementation of any legislation. How do the Scheduled Castes respondents feel about the role of the Police ? Are they effective in their role-performance ? These issues are discussed in brief with the help of data presented in Table 2.13.

It is observed that half of the respondents feel that the Police is not at all effective in implementing the PCR Act. To many of them, it is because of their inaction and biased attitudes that the caste-Hindus take advantage inspite of the measures of the State and the Law. There are more respondents in Andhra and Karnataka sharing this view than the

TABLE 2.12

Opinion of the Non-Scheduled Caste Respondents About the Complaints Lodged by the Scheduled Caste Victims

States	*Always false*		*Sometimes false*		*Real*		*Total*	
	N	%	*N*	%	*N*	%	*N*	%
Karnataka	10	13.3	25	33.3	40	53.4	75	100.0
Tamil Nadu	5	10.0	10	20.0	35	70.0	50	100.0
Andhra Pradesh	10	20.0	12	24.0	28	56.0	50	100.0
Kerala	—	—	5	20.0	20	80.0	25	100.0
Total	25	12.5	52	26.0	123	61.5	200	100.0

TABLE 2.13

Opinion of Scheduled Caste Respondents About Effectiveness of Police Officers.

States	*Very effective*		*Moderately effective*		*Not at all effective*		*Total*	
	N	%	*N*	%	*N*	%	*N*	%
Karnataka	15	10.0	45	30.0	90	60.0	150	100.0
Tamil Nadu	20	20.0	40	20.0	40	40.0	100	100.0
Andhra Pradesh	10	10.0	20	20.0	70	70.0	100	100.0
Kerala	30	60.0	20	40.0	—	—	50	100.0
Total	75	18.7	125	31.3	200	50.0	400	100.0

respondents of Tamil Nadu. Kerala is totally free from this criticism. None of the Kerala respondents say that the Police is ineffective.

Though the remaining half of the respondents say in general that the Police is effective, not all of them are of similar opinion. There is a divided opinion about the degree of effectiveness. It is seen that in general only 19% of the Police is always effective. Kerala tops with 60%. The responses of this type are very poor in other States. More of Karnataka and Andhra Pradesh respondents feel that the role of the Police is moderately effective than very effective.

Reasons for Ineffective Role

The respondents were asked to give reasons, if they could, as to why the Police become ineffective. All the respondents were able to give some reasons. This situation is presented in Table 2.14.

Four social variables are found in the Table, namely caste, class, religion and pressure. Caste accounts for the highest percentage of 57. Respondents whether in or outside the phenomenon of caste do feel that it is caste of the Police and the caste of the Hindus that generally guide the Police in their duty. If the Police officer is a caste-Hindu he is likely though not necessarily, to shield the caste-Hindu. Sometimes even the Scheduled Caste officers hesitate to initiate immediate action because of the fear of the powerful caste Hindus.

Though a sizeable number of the Scheduled Castes in all the States refer to the caste factor, Kerala tops with 80% and Tamil Nadu with the least, 50%. The majority of respondents in Karnataka as well as Andhra Pradesh quote this factor.

Class factor is not that significant. Only 19% respondents in general refer to this. Kerala accounts for the lowest percentage and Tamil Nadu the highest. In other words, wherever

TABLE 2.14

Factors Responsible for the Ineffective Performance of the Officers, According to Scheduled Caste Respondents

States	*Caste*		*Class*		*Religion*		*Pressure*		*Total*	
	N	%	*N*	%	*N*	%	*N*	%	*N*	%
Karnataka	80	53.3	30	20.1	20	13.3	20	13.3	150	100.0
Tamil Nadu	50	50.0	25	25.0	10	10.0	15	15.0	100	100.0
Andhra Pradesh	60	60.0	15	15.0	10	10.0	15	15.0	100	100.0
Kerala	40	80.0	5	10.0	—	—	5	10.0	50	100.0
Total	230	57.5	75	18.7	40	10.0	55	13.8	400	100.0

caste factor is dominant, class factor is less pronounced, even though quite often caste and class combination is not ruled out in suppressing the Scheduled Castes.

Only 10% respondents say that religious background of the Police is a force to be reckoned with. While none in Kerala bring religion into picture, in all other States a small percentage of respondents do attribute the role of the Police to religious affiliation.

Pressure from the higher officers and politicians is also referred to by the respondents, but to a small extent. In general 14% say that the Police will be under pressure and hence even if they are good, they become ineffective. "Even Scheduled Castes Police constable cannot give us protection, Sir, because they are pressurised", was the reaction of some respondents. In Kerala 10% respondents speak of pressure and in other States, the precentage is slightly higher.

About Police

As explained elsewhere, police is both the crucial and controversial subject. What is required is an objective assessment of their role in situations of extreme sensitiveness. What opinion do the Non-Scheduled Caste respondents hold about the Police ? Answer to this is furnished with the help of data presented in Table 2.15.

It is observed from the table that the opinion is sharply divided among the respondents. Those who say that the role of the Police is 'fair' constitute 40%. A slightly higher percentage of the respondents express that the Police is biased in favour of the Caste Hindus. There are also some respondents accounting for 17.5% saying that the Police is biased in favour of the Scheduled Castes.

As usual, the main reason for this varying opinion is that generally caste-Hindus are in favour of the Police and the others

TABLE 2.15

Opinion of the Non-Scheduled Caste respondents about the role of the police.

States	*Biased in favour of Caste Hindus*		*Biased in favour of S. Castes*		*Fair*		*Total*	
	N	%	*N*	%	*N*	%	*N*	%
Karnataka	25	33.3	15	20.0	35	46.7	75	100.0
Tamil Nadu	20	40.0	10	20.0	20	40.0	50	100.0
Andhra Pradesh	30	60.0	10	20.0	10	20.0	50	100.0
Kerala	10	40.0	—	—	15	60.0	25	100.0
Total	85	42.5	35	17.5	80	40.0	200	100.0

are not. In other words, opinion of the respondents is subjected to their own caste affiliation.

Opinion of Non-Scheduled Castes

The popular notion about the role of the activities is that they create problems and do lot of damage to the Society. This attitude needs to be examined carefully. Therefore, a few questions were put to the non-Scheduled Caste respondents. Table 2.16 has relevant data.

It is seen from the Table that the majority of these respondents (59.5%) hold the view that the activists are helpful in correcting the erring society. The position remains the same among the respondents of all the four States, with of course variation in the percentages. Kerala tops with 80% expressing this view. Karnataka accounts for the lowest percentage of 53. Tamil Nadu and Andhra Pradesh are in between.

Those who feel that they are harmful account for just 21.5%. These respondents say that they unnecessarily provoke the Scheduled Castes and encourage them to raise against the Caste-Hindus. This opinion is shared by about one-fourth of the respondents of all the States excepting Kerala. None of the respondents of Kerala hold this view.

The rest of the respondents remain neutral as they either do not have sufficient experience to express their opinion on this issue or they do not want to say.

Facilities of the State

The victims of untouchablity are often exposed to various handicaps after the offence is commited by the anti-Scheduled Caste-Hindus. They need immediate as well as future facilities. Some of these are legal aid, medical aid, protection and job-security, according to the Scheduled Caste respondents. The relevant data are presented in Table 2.17.

Legal aid is provided according to 67% respondents in general. Every State has set up Legal Aid Board and its

TABLE 2.16

Opinion of the Non-Schedule Castes Respondents About the Role of Activists.

States	Helpful		Harmful		Neutral		Total	
	N	%	N	%	N	%	N	%
Karnataka	40	53.3	20	26.7	15	20.0	75	100.0
Tamil Nadu	30	60.0	12	24.0	8	16.0	50	100.0
Andhra Pradesh	29	58.0	11	22.0	10	20.0	50	100.0
Kerala	20	80.0	—	—	5	20.0	25	100.0
Total	119	59.5	43	21.5	38	19.0	200	100.0

TABLE 2.17

Facilities Provided by the State to the Victims, According to Scheduled Caste Respondents

State	*Legal aid*		*Medical aid*		*Protection*		*Job security*	
	N	*%*	*N*	*%*	*N*	*%*	*N*	*%*
Karnataka N=150	100	66.7	110	73.3	40	26.7	30	20.0
Tamil Nadu N=100	70	70.0	90	90.0	60	60.0	40	40.0
Andhra Pradesh N=100	60	60.0	70	70.0	30	30.0	25	25.0
Kerala N=50	40	80.0	40	80.0	45	90.0	45	90.0
Total N=400	270	67.5	310	77.5	175	43.7	140	35.0

awareness is being spread. The vast majority of the Scheduled Caste respondents are no doubt not aware of the Legal Aid Boards. But they say that legal aid is provided. This is the position in all the States. Kerala tops with 80% and Andhra-Pradesh has the lowest percentage of 60.

Medical aid is the immediate need. Much depends upon the locally available resources for this. Seventy seven per cent respondents say that they get medical aid. This is so in all the States. Tamil Nadu tops with 90% and Andhra Pradesh is the lowest with 70%. But the respondents also said that private doctors and clinics in the nearby towns refuse to entertain them. Thus they have to be taken from place to place. Government hospitals do entertain, but generally very reluctantly.

But so far as protection is concerned, the response of the State seems to be not encouraging. Only 44% respondents say that they get protection from the State against the oppressive Caste-Hindus. If timely protection is not ensured, huts of the Scheduled Castes will be set on fire, their crops will be destroyed and they will be beaten up mercilessly, according to the respondents. "Sir, we hesitate to lodge complaint. We know what happens to us afterwards. The Caste-Hindus have every thing at their command. Police belongs to them. Who will help us ? This is how some knowledgeable respondents reacted.

The position changes sharply from State to State. Kerala respondents say by a vast majority of 90% that the State gives protection to the victim. Tamil Nadu follows next with 60%. But Karnataka and Andhra Pradesh are far behind. Only around one-fourths of these respondents gave the information that the State gives them protection.

Another reason which compels the Scheduled Castes to remain silent whenever they are insulted, humiliated and assaulted is the fear of losing jobs. They are all mostly working on the farms of the Caste-Hindus. They will be thrown out of jobs. Therefore, some of them do feel that they should have job security (35%). In Kerala 90% respondents said so. It is not that Kerala has the problem. What they say is that job security is a relevant social security measure. Kerala has ensured this and therefore based on their experience, Kerala respondents offer this suggestion. The situation is slightly better in Tamil Nadu compared to Karnataka or Andhra Pradesh. These States have failed very badly.

Availability of Witnesses

Availability of witnesses is a major problem. When this issue was raised with the respondents, they could give their views as presented in Table 2.18.

Nearly 17% respondents in general say that witnesses will not be available at all. While in Kerala there is no such problem, in other States this view prevails to some extent. It is Andhra Pradesh that 30% respondents say so.

Though the rest say that witnesses are available, even here there is lot of variation. About 27% respondents in general say that witnesses are always available. In Kerala and Tamil Nadu 40% are of this view, whereas in Karnataka and Kerala the position is worse with 20%.

Thirty seven percent say that witnesses are mostly available. Statewise position in Karnataka and Kerala account for a little more than 40%. Eighteen per cent in general say that witnesses are sometimes available. The position varies from State to State, though in small degrees.

Problems of Witnesses

One of the major reasons for failure of cases in the courts is non-availability of witnesses. These witnesses have to speak against the Caste-Hindus. The Scheduled Caste respondents were asked to give reasons for not getting witnesses. This is provided in Table 2.19.

TABLE 2.18

Availability of Witnesses, according to the Scheduled Castes Respondents

States	*Always available*		*Mostly available*		*Sometimes available*		*Not at all available*		*Total*	
	N	%	*N*	%	*N*	%	*N*	%	*N*	%
Karnataka	30	20.0	70	46.7	22	14.7	28	18.6	150	100.0
Tamil Nadu	40	40.0	31	31.0	20	20.0	9	9.0	100	100.0
Andhra Pradesh	20	20.0	26	26.0	24	24.0	30	30.0	100	100.0
Kerala	20	40.0	21	42.0	9	18.0	—	—	50	100.0
Total	110	27.5	148	37.7	75	18.7	67	16.8	400	100.0

TABLE 2.19

Reasons for not getting witnesses easily, according to the Scheduled Caste Respondents

States	Fear of Caste Hindus		Loss of job		Loss of Income		Expensive	
	N	%	N	%	N	%	N	%
Karnataka N=150	70	46.7	51	34.0	60	40.0	30	20.0
Tamil Nadu N=100	52	52.0	51	51.0	40	40.0	25	25.0
Andhra Pradesh N=100	70	70.0	40	40.0	46	46.0	30	30.0
Kerala N=50	10	20.0	20	40.0	15	30.0	15	30.0
Total N=400	202	50.5	162	40.5	161	40.2	100	25.0

The four reasons are : fear of Caste-Hindus, loss of jobs, loss of income and cost. As seen from the table fear of the caste-Hindus is the major reason. About 50% respondents in general give this reason. The Caste-Hindus who are the money lenders, employees etc., threaten them if they dare say anything in the courts. The position is most acute in Andhra Pradesh where 70% respondents say so. The least is in Kerala.

Loss of jobs is another reason which makes the locals hesitate giving evidence before the court. This is easy to comprehend. These poor people, particularly Scheduled Castes, cannot accord the risk. In general 40% respondents say so. This is the position in all the States. There is no significant difference among them.

Connected with loss of jobs, is the fear of loss of income. The respondents are not happy with the administration so far as payment of DA/TA is concerned. Maintenance of the family is the most important concern of the witnesses.

One-fourth of the respondents in general, and about that in relation to various States say that bearing witness results in heavy cost. Expensiveness prevents them from going to distant towns and cities to give evidence. "Why should we undertake all these risks and losses. We know ultimately our people suffer. Courts and police will not help us".

Trust

Another crucial issue raised with the Scheduled Castes is 'whom do you trust' in protection of your rights. Their answers are presented in Table 2.20. It is observed that majority of them in general and at State level have trust in the Dalit Sangharsh Samities (DSS) or similar organizations. This is the position in different States. In Karnataka 63% respondents have faith in D.S.S. In other States also Dalit Organizations are quoted frequently.

Only 18% have faith in the Police force in general. This is more or less the position in all the States. About one-fourth of

TABLE 2.20

Whom do the Scheduled Castes Trust ?

States	*Police*		*Politicians*		*D.S.S.*		*Total*	
	N	%	*N*	%	*N*	%	*N*	%
Karnataka	30	20.0	25	16.7	95	83.3	150	100.0
Tamil Nadu	15	15.0	35	35.0	50	50.0	100	100.0
Andhra Pradesh	16	16.0	29	29.0	55	55.0	100	100.0
Kerala	12	24.0	14	28.0	24	48.0	50	100.0
Total 400	73	18.0	103	25.8	224	56.0	400	100.0

the total respondents in general have trust in the politicians. Tamil Nadu accounts for the highest percentage and Karnataka has the lowest percentage.

Suggestions

Despite differing opinion on the complaints lodged by the victims, the non-Scheduled Caste respondents do offer some suggestions for better implementation of the measures of the State. Their suggestions are presented in Table 2.21.

In general, a vast majority with 97% respondents feel that improvement of the economic conditions should be taken up on priority basis. This followed by 90% respondents who say that educating the people about the problems and measures of the State would go a long way. There are about 72% respondents who want severe punishment to be given to the guilty Hindus. That the officers concerned should be punished for their negligence on spathy was suggested by 62.5% respondents.

Statewise position is more or less similar. While 100% respondents of Tamil Nadu, Andhra Pradesh and Kerala desire real improvement in the economic conditions of the Scheduled Castes, 93% of Karnataka respondents suggest this. While 100% Kerala respondents want the guilty to be punished and people to be educated, there is a slightly lower percentage in the other States. A vast majority of all the respondents of all these States want the guilty to be punished.

Another suggestion that the concerned officers should be punished was offered by 100% to 50% of the respondents of these States.

TABLE 2.21

Suggestions of the Non-Scheduled Caste Respondents for better implentation of the measures of the State

States	*Punish Indifference Officers*		*Educate People*		*Improve Economic Conditions of Scheduled Castes*		*Punish the guilty Hindus*	
	N	%	*N*	%	*N*	%	*N*	%
Karnataka N=50	45	60.0	65	86.7	70	93.3	50	66.7
Tamil Nadu N=50	30	85.7	45	90.0	50	100.0	35	70.0
Andhra Pradesh N=50	25	50.0	45	90.0	50	100.0	40	80.0
Kerala N=25	25	100.0	25	100.0	25	100.0	20	80.0
Total N=100	125	62.5	180	90.0	195	97.5	145	72.5

CHAPTER III

Activists and the PCR Act

The significance of the emergence of the activists has already been touched in brief in the introductory Chapter. Since the activists are all literates, some of them having had higher education, their perception and role would naturally lend valuable support. Hence, the present Chapter centres round their role.

The variables included for the purpose mentioned above are :

1. Areas of tensions and conflicts,
2. Awareness of legislations,
3. Sources of awareness of PCR Act,
4. Extent of knowledge about PCR Act,
5. Awareness of measures of the State,
6. Knowledge and reaction to CRE Cell,
7. Opinion about Police and administrative officers and usefulness of the system,

8. Opinion about judiciary and political parties, peace committees,
9. Opinion about adequacy and suggestions for improvement of the measures.

Areas of Tensions and Conflicts

It was desirable to know from the activists the various areas of tensions and conflicts arising out of traditional practices of discrimination by the caste-Hindus and the emergence of organized efforts to challenge these traditions. Table 3.1 has relevant information.

There are seven areas, namely : entry into temples, religious processions, land grants, challenge to caste-Hindus, entry into hotels, social discrimination and exploitation of women.

About 65% activists in general say that temple entry is still an area of tension and conflicts. According to them, not all Scheduled Castes are keen on temple entry. If the caste-Hindus do not allow us to enter the temples, it means they do not consider us as Hindus. But we are interested to enter the temples, only as a challenge, remarked some activists. Excepting Kerala where only one-fourth of the respondents mention this, in all other States the vast majority expresses this opinion. Andhra Pradesh tops with 78%.

Religious procession is another irritating factor. Tensions and conflicts occur both when the Scheduled Castes take out processions in the caste-Hindu areas and when the try to join the processions taken out by the caste-Hindus. This view is shared by 67% activists in general and a vast majority in other States excepting in Kerala where the number is small.

Whenever the Government grants lands to the Scheduled Castes under various schemes, attempts are made subsequently by some caste-Hindus to deprive them of the lands either by force or by inducement. A little more than one third of the respondents share this view in general. Andhra Pradesh

TABLE 3.1

Areas of tensions and conflicts, according to the activists

States	*Entry into temple*		*Religious Procession*	
	N	%	*N*	%
1	2	3	4	5
Karnataka N=110	80	72.7	85	77.3
Tamil Nadu N=45	30	66.7	30	66.7
Andhra Pradesh N=40	35	77.8	35	77.8
Kerala N=40	10	25.0	10	25.0
Total N=240	155	64.6	160	66.7

Land grant		*Challenge to caste Hindus*		*Hotel*		*Social discrimination*		*Exploiting Women*	
N	%	*N*	%	*N*	%	*N*	%	*N*	%
6	7	8	9	10	11	12	13	14	15
40	36.4	85	77.3	70	63.6	90	81.8	30	27.3
10	22.2	25	55.6	35	77.8	35	77.8	10	22.2
30	66.7	40	88.8	40	88.8	40	88.8	25	55.6
8	20	6	15	8	20	5	12.5	—	—
88	36.7	151	65	153	63.7	170	71.0	65	27.1

accounts for the highest percentage of 67 and Kerala has just 20%.

The Hindu traditional attitudes are generally based on the axis of purity and pollution. The old age traditions cannot be disrespected. In fact, any attempt to challenge this is taken to be an attempt to break the traditions and disrespect the established system. Sixty five per cent respondents in general hold this view. They were emphatic by quoting instances of the caste-Hindus creating problems to them. The largest number comes from Andhra Pradesh and the smallest from Kerala with 89 and 15%. Tamil Nadu is better than Karnataka.

Hotel entry is still a problem. Sixty four per cent respondents in general say that either they are not allowed to enter the hotels at all or partial restrictions are imposed.

In Kerala it is very minimum (20%). Andhra tops with 89%. In Karnataka and Tamil Nadu also hotel entry is a problem according to a vast majority.

Social discrimination in various other forms is also reported by 71% respondents in general. Excepting in Kerala where the percentage is negligible, in all other States more than three-fourth of the respondents say so. Andhra Pradesh tops with 89%, Tamil Nadu is better than Karnataka.

Exploitation of women in various forms is referred to by about one-fourth of the respondents in general. While there is none in Kerala to say so, Andhra Pradesh accounts for 56%. Karnataka and Tamil Nadu have about one-fourth of the respondents sharing this view.

Awareness of Legislations

Unlike in the case of the Scheduled Caste respondents and to some extent in the case of the Non-Scheduled Caste, it could be expected that the activists are aware of various legislations solely enacted to protect the interest of the Scheduled Caste people. Hence, this issue was discussed with them. Necessary data are presented in Table 3.2.

It is seen that the majority of them constituting 62% are aware of the Untouchability Offences Act. Even among the various States, the position is quite encouraging with Kerala accounting for the highest percentage of 75. Karnataka stands last, but has a little more than half of the activists having awareness. Of course, Tamil Nadu and Andhra activists have an edge over the activists of Karnataka.

Awareness of PCR Act is much better among the activists in general and also activists of the four States. Nearly three-fourth of the activists are aware of this in general. State-wise speaking, it is seen that Kerala tops with 87%. The remaining States also present an encouraging position. Even though Karnataka is behind Tamil Nadu and Andhra Pradesh, it has nearly two-third of the activists having awareness.

However, the situation is altogether different in regard to the Atrocities Act. In general it is just 19% activities who are aware of this. Surprisingly Tamil Nadu has an edge over Kerala. There is not much difference between Karnataka and Andhra Pradesh.

Sources of Awareness

The various sources of awareness of these legislations are indicated in Table 3.3. The best source is social conflicts. A vast majority constituting 85% quote this source. There is almost similar opinion among the activists of all the states. The next best source is friends. This accounts for 73% in general. While Kerala tops with 86%, Andhra Pradesh has 67%. In between are Karnataka and Tamil Nadu.

Of the other sources, namely 'newspapers', 'radio', T.V. and government, it is seen that government source is the best with 47% in general. Kerala accounts for the highest percentage and Andhra Pradesh has the lowest. T.V. comes next with

TABLE 3.2

Awareness of legislations among the Activists

States	Untouchability Offences Act			
	Aware		Not Aware	
	N	%	N	%
1	2	3	4	5
Karnataka N=110	60	54.5	50	45.5
Tamil Nadu N=45	30	66.7	15	33.3
Andhra Pradesh N=45	29	64.4	16	35.5
Kerala N=40	30	75	10	25
Total N=240	149	62.1	91	38.0

Protection of Civil Rights Act				*SC/ST Abolition of Actrocities Act*			
Aware		*Not Aware*		*Aware*		*Not Aware*	
N	%	*N*	%	*N*	%	*N*	%
6	7	8	9	10	11	12	13
70	63.3	40	36.4	20	18.2	90	81.2
35	77.8	10	22.2	10	22.2	35	77.8
30	66.7	15	33.3	8	17.8	37	82.2
35	87.5	5	12.5	8	20	32	80
170	71.0	70	29.2	46	19.2	194	81.0

TABLE 3.3

Sources of awareness of P.C.R. Act among the Activists

States	*News paper*		*Radio*	
	N	%	*N*	%
1	2	3	4	5
Karnataka N=70	10	14.3	15	21.0
Tamil Nadu N=35	8	23.0	9	26.0
Andhra Pradesh N=30	7	23.3	6	20
Kerala N=35	10	28.6	12	34.3
Total N=170	35	21.0	42	25.0

T.V.		Friends		Government		Social conflicts	
N	%	*N*	%	*N*	%	*N*	%
6	7	8	9	10	11	12	13
20	28.6	50	71.4	30	43.0	60	85.6
10	28.6	25	71.4	19	54.2	30	86.0
8	26.7	20	66.7	11	36.7	25	83.3
14	40	30	86	20	57.1	30	86
52	31	120	73.5	80	47	145	85.3

31% in general and in all the other States also it is about 25% excepting in Kerala where it is 40%. Next is radio with 25% in general and newspaper 21%. This is the position in all the states too. Kerala stands first in both cases.

Extent of Knowledge

Apart from having heard of the legislations and the various sources, what is more relevant is the extent of knowledge that the activists have. If they are well informed, they in turn can take the message to the people and create awareness. Table 3.4 has information on this.

Those who have full knowledge of the PCR Act account for just 25% in general and this is the position in all the States excepting small variations in the percentage. Kerala and Tamil Nadu are on par and Karnataka is behind Andhra Pradesh. The mostly knowledgeable category accounts for 30% in general. Even here Kerala and Tamil Nadu are on par with 43%. Karnataka is much better than Andhra Pradesh.

Those who have 'partial knowledge' are to the extent of 39% in general. Here Karnataka accounts for 43% and Andhra Pradesh has a slightly higher percentage. Kerala and Tamil Nadu are on par.

From all counts, Kerala stands first and Andhra Pradesh last so far as the extent of knowledge possessed is concerned.

Awareness of Measures

The State has formulated various measures to ensure effective implementation of the Act. This is discussed in the introductory Chapter and elsewhere. What is the extent of awareness among the activists ? This is discussed in brief here with the help of the data presented in Table 3.5.

Among all these measures, CRE Cell is known to a very large number accounting for as high as 92% in general. While in Kerala 100% activists are aware of this, even in other States about 90% are aware of this Cell.

TABLE 3.4

Extent of the knowledge about PCR Act among the activists

States	*Fully Knowledgeable*		*Mostly Knowledgeable*		*Partly Knowledgeable*		*Total*	
	N	*%*	*N*	*%*	*N*	*%*	*N*	*%*
Karnataka	15	21.4	25	36.0	30	43.0	70	100.0
Tamil Nadu	10	29.0	15	43.0	10	28.6	35	100.0
Andhra Pradesh	8	27.0	6	20.0	16	53.3	30	100.0
Kerala	10	29.0	15	43.0	10	28.6	35	100.0
Total	43	25.3	61	30.0	66	39.0	170	100.0

TABLE 3.5

Awareness of certain measures of the State among the Scheduled Caste activists.

States	CRE Cell				Mobile Courts			
	Aware		Not Aware		Aware		Not Aware	
	N	%	N	%	N	%	N	%
1	2	3	4	5	6	7	8	9
Karnataka N=110	100	90.9	10	9.1	20	18.2	90	81.8
Tamil Nadu N=45	40	88.9	5	11.1	10	22.2	35	77.8
Andhra Pradesh N=45	40	88.9	5	11.1	7	15.6	38	84.4
Kerala N=40	40	100.0	—	—	13	32.5	27	67.5
Total N=240	200	91.7	20	8.3	50	20.8	190	79.2

Special Court				*Summary Trial*				*Collective Fine*			
Aware		*Not Aware*		*Aware*		*Not Aware*		*Aware*		*Not Aware*	
N	%	*N*	%	*N*	%	*N*	%	*N*	%	*N*	%
10	11	12	13	14	15	16	17	18	19	20	21
18	16.4	92	83.6	10	9.1	100	90.9	6	5.4	104	94.6
8	17.8	37	82.2	5	11.1	40	88.9	7	15.6	38	84.4
8	17.8	37	82.2	3	6.7	42	93.3	3	6.7	42	93.3
14	35.0	26	65.0	9	22.5	31	77.5	3	7.5	37	92.5
48	20.0	192	80.0	27	11.2	213	88.8	19	7.9	221	92.1

But the other measures of the States are poorly known. Mobile courts are known to just 21% in general. Even in Kerala awareness is to the extent of 32%. The lowest percentage is in the case of Andhra Pradesh (16%). Special courts are known in general to 20% activists. Kerala accounts for 35% and the lowest percentage is in Karnataka. But Tamil Nadu and Andhra Pradesh are not much better than Karnataka.

Summary trial is known to a very negligible number of activists (11%) in general. While in Kerala it is 22%, the least is in Andhra Pradesh (7%). Collective fine is known to still smaller number in general (8%). Surprisingly, Tamil Nadu has the highest percentage of 16 and the lowest is in Karnataka (5%). Kerala has poor performance here.

Period of Awareness of Cell

Table 3.6 has information on the period of awareness of the CRE Cell among the activists. In general majority of the respondents (55%) have known only during the last 5 years. This is the position among the different States excepting Kerala. It is only in Kerala that majority have known before 5 years.

Those who have known the Cell 10 years and above constitute a small percentage in general as well as in relation to the States. Excepting Kerala where one-fourth have known during this period, the performance of other State is poor. Those who have known between 5 and 10 years constitute a little more than one-fourth in general. This is the position in Karnataka, Tamil Nadu and Andhra Pradesh. But Kerala presents a different picture. A little more than 50% have known it during this period.

Thus, excepting in the case of Kerala in all the other States, awareness is generally during the last five years only.

Sources of Information

The various sources of information about CRE Cell are

TABLE 3.6

Period since when CRE Cell is known to the activisits

States	*10 years ago*		*5-10 years*		*Less than 5 years*		*Total*	
	N	*%*	*N*	*%*	*N*	*%*	*N*	*%*
Karnataka	15	15.0	25	25.0	60	60.0	100	100.0
Tamil Nadu	5	12.5	10	25.0	25	62.5	40	100.0
Andhra Pradesh	4	10.0	9	22.5	27	67.5	40	100.0
Kerala	10	25.0	21	52.5	9	22.5	40	100.0
Total	34	15.4	65	29.5	121	55.0	220	100.0

indicated in Table 3.7. There are four sources, namely newspaper, radio/TV, friends and conflicting situation. Conflicting situation is the most significant source. Eighty two per cent activists have given this source in general. Even State wise, this is the most frequented source. In Kerala it is 100% and in the remaining States, it is 75 to 80%.

'Friends' account for the next best source with 54%. In Kerala, it is to the extent of 75%. Karnataka and Andhra Pradesh are behind Tamil Nadu. Radio and T.V. account for 36% in general. In Karnataka it is to the extent of 40%. Kerala has only 25%. So for as newspaper is concerned, a little more than one-fourth in general and also State wise indicate this source.

Opinion on CRE Cell

The activists are divided in their opinion on CRE Cell as noted in Table 3.8. It is seen that 48% activists feel that the Cell is not at all effective. In relation to the various States the position is that excepting Kerala, in the remaining three States this is the feeling expressed by the majority.

Only 15% activists in general feel that the Cell is very effective. But when the position in each State is considered, it is seen that it is only in Kerala that 35% have said so. In the remaining States the situation is very poor. Nearly 37% activists in general say that the Cell is moderately effective. It is in Kerala that the majority speak in favour of the Cell (60%). The rest of the States account for about 30%.

Opinion About Administrative Officers

Much of the success of CRE Cell depends upon the interest and committment that the administration has. The various officers at the Taluk as well as District levels are expected to play a vital role in mitigating the problems in the Scheduled castes. There are allegations that these officers have generally failed in their duty. What do the activists say about this ? This is discussed with the help of data presented in Table 3.9.

TABLE 3.7

Sources of information about CRE Cell, according to the activists

States	*News paper*		*Radio / TV*		*Friends*		*Conflicting situation*	
	N	*%*	*N*	*%*	*N*	*%*	*N*	*%*
1	2	3	4	5	6	7	8	9
Karnataka N=100	30	30.0	40	40 0	45	45.0	80	80.0
Tamil Nadu N=40	10	25.0	15	37.5	25	62.5	30	75.0
Andhra Pradesh N–40	10	25.0	15	37.5	20	50.0	30	75.0
Kerala N=40	10	25 0	10	25.0	30	75.0	40	100.0
Total N=220	60	27.3	80	36.4	120	54.5	180	81.8

TABLE 3.8

Opinion of activists on CRE Cell

States	*Very effective* N	%	*Moderately effective* N	%	*Not at all effective* N	%	*Total* N	%
Karnataka	10	10.0	30	30.0	60	60.0	100	100.0
Tamil Nadu	5	12.5	15	37.5	20	50.0	40	100.0
Andhra Pradesh	4	10.0	12	30.0	24	60.0	40	100.0
Kerala	14	35.0	24	60.0	2	5.0	40	100.0
Total	33	15.0	81	36.8	106	48.2	220	100.0

Three extreme types of answers are furnished by the activists. These are : Officers are interested, indifferent and hostile. Those who are hostile contribute only 21% in general. This is the trend in all the States excepting Kerala. In Kerala, this type of feeling is almost negligible.

Nearly 41% respondents in general said that the Officers are interested in rendering real service to the Scheduled castes in distress. If at all there is a gap between what they intend and what they do, it is mostly because of the interference by the politicians, according to the respondents. But the activists also admit that there are some officers who have no interest at all.

Indifference of the officers is referred to by 38% respondents. These are the officers who are neither hostile nor interested. For various reasons they remain indifferent. Such officers are in all the States. But the respondents of Kerala do not quote this by a large number. Only 20% say so. It is in Karnataka and Andhra Pradesh that there is a larger number expressing this feeling. In Tamil Nadu also there is a lower percentage.

Opinion About Usefulness

Whether any individual officer or group of officers are responsible for the present situation or the system as such is accountable ? The opinion of the respondents on this issue was assessed. Relevant data are presented in Table 3.10.

The opinion of the activists is more or less equally divided on this issue. Those who say that the present system is useful constitute just 31% in general. It is in Kerala that three-fourths of the activists hold the view that the system is useful. In other States, a vast majority does not agree.

Those who say that the system is not useful are to the extent of 38% in general. In Andhra Pradesh the position is the worst. About 56% say that the system is not useful. Even in Kerala one-fourth of them say so.

TABLE 3.9

Opinion of the activists about administrative officers

States	*Interested*		*Indifferent*		*Hostile*		*Total*	
	N	%	*N*	%	*N*	%	*N*	%
Karnataka	31	28.2	49	44.5	30	27.3	110	100.0
Tamil Nadu	22	48.9	14	31.1	9	20.0	45	100.0
Andhra Pradesh	15	33.4	20	44.4	10	22.2	45	100.0
Kerala	30	75.0	8	20.0	2	5.0	40	100.0
Total	98	40.8	91	37.9	51	21.3	240	100.0

TABLE 3.10

Opinion about usefulness of the present system

States	*Useful*		*Not Useful*		*Harmful*		*Total*	
	N	%	*N*	%	*N*	%	*N*	%
Karnataka	20	18.2	42	38.2	48	43.6	110	100.0
Tamil Nadu	15	33.3	15	33.3	15	33.4	45	100.0
Andhra Pradesh	10	22.2	25	55.6	10	22.2	45	100.0
Kerala	30	75.0	10	25.0	—	—	40	100.0
Total	75	31.2	92	38.3	73	30.5	240	100.0

There is a direct question, whether the system is harmful. In general 30% say so. But in Kerala none accepts this view. In Karnataka 44% say that the system is harmful. Tamil Nadu and Andhra Pradesh activists also hold this view, but account for a lower percentage.

About Police Officers

Opinion of the activists about the Police officers is more or less equally divided as seen in Table 3.11. In general, 33% say that no Police officers are not at all effective. Excepting in Kerala, where the percentage is very low, in all the other States, there is a sizeable number holding this view. While in Karnataka it is 41%, Tamil Nadu and Andhra Pradesh account for slightly reduced percentage.

This means that 67% activists hold the view that the Police Officers are effective. But even here there are two groups. Those who say the Police officers are very effective account for 31% in general. Kerala tops with 50% holding this view. Andhra Pradesh has the lowest percentage. Those who hold the view that these officers are moderately effective account for 35% in general. While in Andhra Pradesh it is to the extent of 44%, other States account for a relatively lower percentage.

Another interesting feature is that Kerala tops among those who say that the Police officers are very effective. Andhra Pradesh stands first among those who say Police officers are moderately effective. Karnataka leads others saying that the Police officers are not at all effective.

Sincere Hindu Officers

The activists were asked to say who among the Hindu Officers are sincere in implementing the PCR Act effectively. Their views are presented in Table 3.12. It is seen that 44% respondents in general as well as that much in relation to the various States feel that Scheduled Castes officers are sincere.

TABLE 3.11

Opinion among the activists about effectiveness of Police Officers.

States	*Very effective*		*Moderately effective*		*Not at all effective*		*Total*	
	N	*%*	*N*	*%*	*N*	*%*	*N*	*%*
Karnataka	30	27.3	35	31.8	45	40.9	110	100.0
Tamil Nadu	15	33.3	15	33.3	15	33.4	45	100.0
Andhra Pradesh	10	22.2	20	44.4	15	33.4	45	100.0
Kerala	20	50.0	15	37.5	5	12.5	40	100.0
Total	75	31.2	85	35.4	80	33.4	240	100.0

TABLE 3.12

Who among the Hindu officers are sincere about effective implementation of PCR Act

States	*Brahmins*		*Non-Brahmin upper Castes*		*Backward castes*		*Scheduled castes*	
	N	%	*N*	%	*N*	%	*N*	%
Karnataka N=110	30	27.3	8	7.3	25	22.7	47	42.7
Tamil Nadu N=45	10	22.2	5	11.1	10	22.2	20	44.5
Andhra Pradesh N=45	8	17.8	5	11.1	12	26.7	20	44.4
Kerala N=40	8	20.0	2	5.0	12	30.0	18	45.0
Total=240	56	23.3	20	8.3	59	24.6	105	43.8

They say that "after all these Scheduled Castes officers are our own men. They too have suffered enough before getting into important jobs. They know how to implement".

When asked why then are not all activists have been unanimous, they said that there are some black sheeps and also those who do not have guts. If the Scheduled Caste officers are weak, not efficient and corrupt, they lack courage and therefore, cannot be effective, according to the activists.

There are three more groups of Hindu officers concerned with this. They are the Brahmins, non-Brahmins upper castes and Backward Castes. In the opinion of the Activists, Brahmin and Backward Castes officers are almost similar. While 25% activists in general say that the Backward Caste officers are sincere, 23% of them express this opinion in the case of the Brahmin officers. Even among the different states, this is the trend.

Various reasons were assigned in group discussions for their opinion. There is a general opposition among the Scheduled Castes to the Brahmins. But the activists say that there are no Brahmins in the rural areas now and there is no problem for them. Brahmin officers have dislike for some non-Brahmin upper caste Hindus. The latter generally trouble the Scheduled Castes. Therefore, the Brahmin officers are more soft towards the Scheduled Caste people.

Similarly, the Backward Caste people are also the sufferers at the hands of the caste-Hindus. There is thus a link between the Scheduled Caste and these people, according to the activists. This therefore, brings Backward Castes closer to the Scheduled Castes. Further the activists say that the Scheduled Castes, minorities and Backward Castes should forge an alliance in their own interest.

The general hatred for the non-Brahmin upper castes is reflected through the opinion of the activists about non-Brahmin upper caste officers. Only 8% activists say that these people are sincere. The position is more or less similar in all the States.

Police Under Pressure

It is generally conceded that in the given Socio-political system, police finds it very hard to act freely and fairly even when it wants to do so. This is because of the tremendous pressure on them. The activists had their own reaction to this, as presented in Table 3.13.

Four types of answers are given here. Those who say that the Police unnecessarily delays when complaints are filed constitute 20%. The Police is expected to act expeditiously as soon as the complaint is lodged by the Police. But delay is caused. Sometimes there would be real causes for the delay. But deliberate delay cannot be ruled out and this is what makes the activists suspect the bonafide of the Police. The positions remains almost similar in all States except in Kerala where the number is very small.

The Police is not expected to effect any compromise when once the complaint is lodged. But in practice, they do so. Such type of intervention will demoralize the victims. This is what the activists say. Twenty three per cent of them say so in general. The position remains similar in all the States including Kerala where the percentage is low.

Changing the nature of offences is alleged by 14% activists. Sometimes cases are booked under Indian Penal Code instead of the PCR Act. This is to avoid severe punishment. Excepting in Kerala, in all the other States, a small number makes this allegation.

The remaining activists constituting 43% say that the Police remains firm and goes ahead with further action. These are the officers who generally do not belong to upper castes and do not yield to pressure.

TABLE 3.13

How Police acts under pressure according to activists

States	*Delay*		*Compromise*		*Change nature of offence*		*Remain firm*	
	N	%	*N*	%	*N*	%	*N*	%
Karnataka N=110	25	22.7	30	27.3	20	18.2	35	31.8
Tamil Nadu N=45	10	22.2	10	22.2	5	11.1	20	44.5
Andhra Pradesh N=45	9	20.0	10	22.2	8	17.8	18	40.0
Kerala N=40	5	12.5	5	12.5	—	—	30	75.0
Total N=240	49	20.4	55	22.9	33	13.7	103	43.0

Suggestions

As pointed out earlier, activists have got fair knowledge of the performance of the officers. Based on this, they were able to offer a few suggestions to improve the performance as well as the accountability of these officers. Their suggestions are indicated in Table 3.14.

The three important suggestions are : Committed officers, punishment and rewards. In general 47% activists say that those who are entrusted with task of effective implementation of the PCR Act should have some commitment to the task. Without commitment, these officers will not be useful. When asked whether such committed officers would be available, the consensus emerged was that in every system there some are who find pleasure and satisfaction by doing their work properly. To another question whether such committed officers are found among the Scheduled Castes and their sympathetic castes, the general feeling was that even among the caste-Hindus there are some officers totally committed.

Two case-studies were presented. One relates to the role of Mr. P.S. Krishnan, a retired IAS Officer. He is not a Scheduled Caste officer. Bat the entire knowledgeable Scheduled Castes hold him in high esteem and have no hesitation to say that he tops all officers including Scheduled Castes officers for the sustained interest. The second case relates to Mr. Srinivas Alva, a retired IPS Officer. He belongs to the dominant caste-Hindus. But he was totally committed to the cause of the Scheduled Castes. As the Deputy Inspector General of Police heading the CRE Cell he did lot of service to the Scheduled Castes in Karnataka. Even today he is remembered with gratitude.

That there is a need to have committed officers is conceded by a sizeable number of the activists. While Kerala tops with 62% in the other States as well, those who make this suggestion account for about 44%.

TABLE 3.14

Suggestions for improving the accountability of the officers, according to the activists

States	Committed officers		Punishment		Reward		Total	
	N	%	*N*	%	*N*	%	*N*	%
Karnataka	50	45.4	25	22.7	35	31.9	110	100.0
Tamil Nadu	20	44.4	10	22.2	15	33.4	45	100.0
Andhra Pradesh	20	44.4	15	33.3	10	22.3	45	100.0
Kerala	25	62.5	5	12.5	10	25.0	40	100.0
Total	115	47.9	55	22.9	70	29.2	240	100.0

Some of the activists are also keen on inflicting punishment on the indifferent and erring officers. Twenty three percent activists hold this view in general. While Kerala activists account for a low percentage here, there were 22 to 33% activists in other States making this suggestion.

Officers with good performance should be rewarded according to 29% activists. Some of them said "Sir, every year we read in newspapers that some administrative and police officers are rewarded for catching thieves, criminals etc. Why the same government does not feel the need to identify and reward officers who have done great service to the Scheduled Castes in order to allow them have their human rights? This means that the State follows double standards". This suggestion for rewards was made by 22 to 33% of activists in all the four States.

Sincerity Among the Groups

Who among the Hindu officers are sincere has already been examined. But in a general frame of various social groups consisting of Muslims, Hindus and Christians, the situation becomes more interesting. This issue was discussed with the activists. Table 3.15 has data on this.

It is seen that of all the groups, Christian officers are sincere, according to 42% activists in general. In relation to the various States, Kerala stands first with 50%. Karnataka and Tamil Nadu activists also say so to a larger extent. But in Andhra Pradesh, the majority of 40% say Muslims are sincere and others come next. In Karnataka 32% say Hindus are sincere and others come next.

It means in Kerala, Christian officers get maximum reference. In Andhra Pradesh Muslim officers are mostly frequented and in Karnataka Hindu officers are quoted more.

About Judiciary

The Scheduted caste respondents were not able to say

TABLE 3.15

Who among the various groups of people are sincere about effective implementation of PCR Act.

States	*Muslims*		*Hindus*		*Christians*		*Total*	
	N	%	*N*	%	*N*	%	*N*	%
Karnataka	30	27.3	35	31.8	45	40.9	110	100.0
Tamil Nadu	15	33.3	10	22.2	20	44.5	45	100.0
Andhra Pradesh	18	40.0	12	26.7	15	33.3	45	100.0
Kerala	11	27.5	9	22.5	20	50.0	40	100.0
Total	74	30.8	66	27.5	100	41.8	240	100.0

anything about the judiciary. It was solely because of their illiteracy and ignorance. The working of the judiciary is generally said to be a major deterrant factor in effective implementation of the PCR Act. Hence, it was felt desirable to test the knowledge of the activists atleast. The replies received by them are presented in Table 3.16.

Thirty one per cent activists in general said that the judges were interested in the cases of the Scheduled caste victims. But for some reasons beyond their control they could not be given enough support by disposing off the cases early, according to the respondents. While 75% of the activists of Kerala said that the judges were interested, among other States, the supporters were extremely limited. In Karnataka it was as low as 18%. Tamil Nadu and Andhra Pradesh just above this.

Indifference of the judges was pointed out by 42% activists in general. While Karnataka stands first with 50%, Kerala activists account for the lowest percentage. A good number of activists of Tamil Nadu and Andhra Pradesh also say so.

A little more than one-fourth of the activists in general pointed out the hostile attitude of the judges. While Karnataka and Andhra Pradesh account for nearly one-third respondents, Tamil Nadu has slightly lower percentage. Kerala accounts for the lowest percentage.

Reasons for Ineffective Performance

Activists were asked to give their reasons for ineffective performance of the officers. Their reasons presented in Table 3.17 are four, namely caste, class, religion and pressure. Those who hold caste factor responsible for ineffective performance of the officers account for 35% in general. Activists of the various States also account for more or less this percentage. Andhra Pradesh activists account for 44% which is the highest percentage.

TABLE 3.16

Opinions of the activists about the judiciary

States	*Interested*		*Indifferent*		*Hostile*		*Total*	
	N	%	*N*	%	*N*	%	*N*	%
Karnataka	20	18.2	55	50.0	35	31.8	110	100.0
Tamil Nadu	15	33.3	20	44.4	10	22.2	45	100.0
Andhra Pradesh	10	22.3	20	44.4	15	33.3	45	100.0
Kerala	30	75.0	5	12.5	5	12.5	40	100.0
Total	75	31.2	100	41.6	65	27.2	240	100.0

TABLE 3.17

Factors responsible for the ineffective performance of the Officers, according to the activists.

States	*Caste*		*Class*		*Religion*		*Pressure*		*Total*	
	N	%	*N*	%	*N*	%	*N*	%	*N*	%
Karnataka	35	31.8	20	18.2	10	9.1	45	40.9	100	100.0
Tamil Nadu	15	33.3	5	11.2	10	22.2	15	33.3	45	100.0
Andhra Pradesh	20	44.5	10	22.2	—	—	15	33.3	45	100.0
Kerala	15	37.5	5	12.5	5	12.5	15	37.5	40	100.0
Total	85	35.4	40	16.7	25	10.4	90	37.5	240	100.0

Class factor is not a major one. Only 17% in general attribute class factor. There is no significant variation among the four States. Religion of the officer is also a factor, but very insignificant. None give this reason in Andhra Pradesh.

Pressure from the higher officers and the politicians is given by 37% respondents. According to them, these officers become helpless when a great deal of pressure is exercised on them by their official superiors and local political leaders. The responses of the activists in various States are more or less similar.

In short in Andhra Pradesh caste and class are major factors. In Karnataka pressure is a major factor. In Tamil Nadu religion is a major factor. In Kerala caste and pressure are major factors.

About Political Parties

The views of the activists in general on the involvement of political parties in effective implementation of the Act are presented in Table 3.18. There is none to say all political parties are sincere in this matter. Only a negligible percentage of activists in Andhra Pradesh say that most of the parties are sincere. In other words, in the remaining States there is none to say this. About 22% activists say that only a few parties are sincere. The responses vary from State to State, but the difference in percentages is only marginal.

That no party is sincere is supported by a little more than three-fourth of the activists. Kerala tops with 82% in other States the percentage varies from 73% to 78%.

Visits by Police Officers

As per the circulars issued by the State Governments, all the Police officers are expected to visit Harijan colonies periodically and submit their reports. The CRE Cell is entrusted

TABLE 3.18

Opinion of the activists about the role of political parties in effective implementation of PCR Act.

States	All parties are sineere		Most of the parties are sincere		Only a few are sincere		None is sincere	
	N	%	N	%	N	%	N	%
Karnataka N=100	—	—	—	—	30	27.3	80	72.7
Tamil Nadu N=45	—	—	—	—	10	22.2	35	77.8
Andhra Pradesh N=45	—	—	3	6.7	7	15.5	35	77.8
Kerala N=40	—	—	—	—	7	17.5	33	82.5
Total N=240	—	—	3	1.2	54	22.5	183	76.3

with this responsibility. When this issue was discussed with the activists, they were able to give their opinion. This is furnished in Table 3.19.

It is seen that only 26% respondents in general say that the police officers visit frequently. When analysed with reference to each State it becomes evident that it is only in Kerala that 55% activists are sure of frequent visits. In other States, the performance is poor.

Forty three per cent respondents say that the Police officers visit Scheduled Caste areas occasionally. The position is more or less similar in Karnataka, Tamil Nadu and Andhra Pradesh. Thirty one per cent say that the Police officers do not visit the areas.

Work Done

The Police officers are expected to render some positive service when they visit the Harijan areas. What work they do their is indicated in Table 3.20. Forty seven per cent respondents say that the officers speak to the Scheduled Caste people and enthuse confidence among them. They try to know their problems and promise to help them. This is the position in relation to the various States. Tamil Nadu tops with 55% and Karnataka has the lowest percentage of 50%. Twenty nine per cent respondents say that false reports are written by these police officers. While there were none to say so in Kerala, 51% of activists in Karnataka say so.

In group discussions, the activists were able to give a lot of evidence in their support that often these officers send the periodical reports without visiting the Harijan areas. Since reports are insisted upon, these are submitted. There is no counter check from the higher circles and therefore, this game goes on.

TABLE 3.19

Visits by police officers to the Harijan areas

States	Frequently		Occasionally		No visits		Total	
	N	%	N	%	N	%	N	%
Karnataka	20	18.2	50	45.4	40	36.4	110	100.0
Tamil Nadu	10	22.2	20	44.4	15	33.4	45	100.0
Andhra Pradesh	10	22.2	21	46.7	14	31.1	45	100.0
Kerala	22	55.0	12	30.0	6	15.0	40	100.0
Total	62	25.8	103	43.0	75	31.2	240	100.0

TABLE 3.20

What is the work done by these officers ?

States	*Talk to Scheduled Caste people*		*Educate the caste Hindus*		*Write false reports*		*Total*	
	N	%	*N*	%	*N*	%	*N*	%
Karnataka	45	40.9	20	18.2	45	40.9	110	100.0
Tamil Nadu	25	55.6	10	22.2	10	22.2	45	100.0
Andhra Pradesh	22	48.9	8	17.8	15	33.3	45	100.0
Kerala	22	55.0	18	45.0	—	—	40	100.0
Total	114	47.5	56	23.3	70	29.2	240	100.0

Peace Committees

Only 25% activists in general say that peace committees are useful as seen in Table 3.21. While in Kerala 65% hold this view, only 14% say so in Karnataka. In between are Tamil Nadu and Andhra. The majority of the respondents in general and in all States except in Kerala say that the peace committees are not useful. Nineteen per cent in general remain neutral. In all States some small number remains netural.

Activists feel that the way in which peace committees are set up only when problems arise would give the impression that the Government is not sincere. Such adhoc committees will not serve any purpose, according to them.

Suggestions to Enthuse Confidence

Four suggestions were offered by the activists to enthuse cofidence among the Scheduled Caste. This is presented in Table 3.22. It is seen that 85% respondents in general desire independent jobs to the Scheduled Castes. It means that they do not want to be under the mercy of the caste-Hindus. This suggestion is given by 100% respondents in Kerala to 79% in Tamil Nadu. In Karnataka and Andhra Pradesh more than 82% respondents hold this view.

Punishment to offenders is also suggested by 69% respondents in general and also by a vast majority in other States. Social integration is desired by 58% in general and 100% in Kerala to 36% in Karnataka.

Another interesting suggestion made by 80% respondents in general is that power should be given to the Scheduled Castes so that they can control the caste-Hindus. While 100% respondents in Kerala say so, the lowest percentage comes for Karnataka. Even here it is 64%. Activists believe that mere lip sympathy will do no good. They pJofusely quote Dr. B.R. Ambedkar's message in this regard.

TABLE 3.21

Opinion of the activists about the Peace Committees

States	*Useful*		*Not useful*		*Neutral*		*Total*	
	N	%	*N*	%	*N*	%	*N*	%
Karnataka	15	13.6	70	63.6	25	22.8	110	100.0
Tamil Nadu	10	22.2	30	66.7	5	11.1	45	100.0
Andhra Pradesh	10	22.2	25	55.6	10	22.2	45	100.0
Kerala	26	65.0	8	20.0	6	15.0	40	100.0
Total	61	25.4	133	55.4	46	19.2	240	100.0

TABLE 3.22

Suggestions to enthuse confidence among the Scheduled Castes

States	*Independent jobs*		*Punishment to the offenders*		*Social integration*		*Power to Scheduled castes*	
	N	*%*	*N*	*%*	*N*	*%*	*N*	*%*
Karnataka N=100	90	81.8	60	54.5	40	36.4	70	63.6
Tamil Nadu N=45	35	77.8	36	80.0	30	66.7	40	88.9
Andhra Pradesh N–45	40	88.9	40	88.9	30	66.7	42	91.1
Kerala N=40	40	100.0	30	75.0	40	100.0	40	100.0
Total N=240	205	85.4	166	69.2	140	58.3	191	79.6

Suggestions to Control Caste-Hindus

When stretched further, the activists were able to give a few suggestions to make the caste-Hindus depend upon them. These are presented in Table 3.23. Location of wells in Harijan areas was suggested by 55% respondents in general. A vast majority of the respondents in all the States excepting in Karnataka made this suggestion.

Fifty per cent in general and a vast majority in all the States excepting Karnataka want location of schools and societies in Harijan areas. Meetings of the officials in Harijan areas was suggested by 35% in general and by a sizeable number in all States excepting Karnataka.

Seventy one per cent activists in general desire that Harijans be made employers of caste-Hindus and land owners. This radical suggestion was made by a vast majority in all States. Even in Karnataka the response was good with 44%. Of course, Kerala tops with 100%. More or less similar number of respondents also suggested that Harijans be made heads of local institutions.

Karnataka respondents were not very enthusiastic because they have developed a feeling that the government will not do anything. According to them, Scheduled Castes have to revolt and get whatever they want.

Facilities of the State

Whether the facilities provided by the State are adequate or not? The reactions of the respondents are presented in Table 3.24. It is observed that the majority constituting 54% say in general that facilities are inadequate. Excepting in Kerala, the position is so in other States.

TABLE 3.23

Suggestions to make Caste-Hindus depend upon the Scheduled Castes

States	*Location of wells in Harijan areas*		*Location of schools and societies in Harijan areas*		*Meetings in Harijan areas*		*Harijans as employers/land owners*		*Harijans as heads of local institutions*	
	N	*%*	*N*	*%*	*N*	*%*	*N*	*%*	*N*	*%*
Karnataka N=110	40	36.4	30	27.3	25	22.7	49	44.5	50	45.4
Tamil Nadu N=45	30	66.7	31	68.9	20	44.4	40	88.9	40	88.9
Andhra Pradesh N=45	30	66.7	29	64.4	19	42.2	41	91.1	40	88.9
Kerala N=40	31	77.5	30	75.0	21	52.5	40	100.0	40	100.0
Total N=240	131	54.6	120	50.0	85	35.4	170	70.8	170	70.8

TABLE 3.24

Adequacy of facilities provided by the State, according to activists

States	*Fully adequate*		*Just adequate*		*Inadequate*		*Total*	
	N	%	*N*	%	*N*	%	*N*	%
Karnataka	15	13.6	25	22.7	70	63.7	110	100.0
Tamil Nadu	10	22.2	11	24.4	24	53.4	45	100.0
Andhra Pradesh	6	13.3	9	20.0	30	66.7	45	100.0
Kerala	14	35.0	20	50.0	6	15.0	40	100.0
Total	45	18.7	65	27.0	130	54.1	240	100.0

Those who say that the facilities are fully adequate constitute just 19% in general and more or less so in the various States excepting in Kerala where 35% respondents say that the facilities are adequate. Twenty seven per cent respondents in general say that the facilities are just adequate. Excepting in Kerala where 50% say so, the position among the respondents of other States is more or less around 20%.

CHAPTER IV

Police and the PCR Act

The expected role of the police in effective implementation of the PCR Act has already been discussed in brief in the introductory chapter. It is conceded that much of the success of any social legislation aimed at correcting the anti-social situations would very much depend upon the role performance of the police. If there is a significant gap beween role-assignment and roleperformance, the result would be unfavourable to the victims of social oppression and exploitation.

In a situation like the conflicts between the untouchable Scheduled Castes and the oppressive caste-Hindus, police is bound to become a subject of controversy. Either way police becomes the target of attack. It could be an allegation of 'police excesses' or 'Police inaction'. Or it could be 'biased police'. This dimension of social relationship is discussed elsewhere too. But in the present Chapter an attempt is made to know from the police itself where it stands in the midst of the controversy.

The various social variables included for the analysis are :

(1) Awareness of the various relevant social legislations.

(2) Knowledge of the police about the reasons for enacting different legislations more or less touching the same victims of social degradation.

(3) Sources of information about the PCR Act.

(4) Extent of the knowledge of the police about the SC/ST Abolition of Atrocities Act and PCR Act.

(5) Sources of information about the offences.

(6) Suggestions for effective implementation of the Act.

(7) Problems faced by the police in the process of implementation of the Act.

(8) Opinion about false allegations.

(9) Police opinion about false-caste certificates.

(10) Suggestions of providing knowledge of the law to the police.

(11) Reasons given by the police for the inefective functioning of the CRE Cell.

These variables are examined with the help of data furnished in the relevant tables. Besides the statistical analysis, attempts have been made to get insights into the problems by having group discussions with the police.

Awareness of Social Legislations

The three legislations that concern the liberty, equality and dignity of the Scheduled Castes people are the Untouchability Offences Act, 1955. The Protection of Civil Rights Act, 1955 and the Scheduled Castes and Scheduled Tribes Abolition of Atrocities Act, 1989. The PCR Act has replaced the Untouchability Offences Act. The main purpose was to sharpen the teeth of the previous legislation and enable it to cover more areas of social discrimination. This had already been mentioned earlier and examined with reference to the Scheduled Castes and Non-Scheduled Castes respondents.

Police involved in arresting problems arising out of violation of these laws are expected to be familiar with them. A few questions were addressed to them. Information obtained are presented in the relevant tables. The first issue relates to the awareness of the above mentioned legislations. The data are presented in table 4.1.

It is seen that a little more than 50% of the police respondents in general are not aware of the Untouchability Offences Act. State-wise position is that the majority of the police in Karnataka and Andhra Pradesh are not aware of this. Whereas the majority of the police in Tamil Nadu and Kerala are aware.

The position is still worse so far as Atrocities Act is concerned. A vast majority of the police in general (67%) as well as in the States are not aware of this law. Andhra is the worst with 76%. Even in a progressive State like Kerala 65% are not aware.

The position of awareness of the PCR Act is quite different. A little more than two-thirds (75.8%) of the police in general are aware of this law. State-wise position is also similar to this. Karnataka State tops with 78% awareness, while Andhra Pradesh has the lowest with 72%. This situation would mean that PCR is best known to the police among all the three legislations.

The situational analysis was further extended to group discussions. Excepting the police officers of and above the rank of Sub-Inspectors, other police personnel are not aware of the Constitutional guarantees for the Scheduled Castes. There was again a general lack of understanding of the years during which the PCR Act and the Atrocities Act were brought into force.

TABLE 4.1

Awareness of the various social legislations on Scheduled Castes—according to Police respondents

States	*Untouchability Offences Act*			
	Aware		*Not Aware*	
	N	%	*N*	%
1	2	3	4	5
Karnataka N=50	21	42.0	29	58.0
Tamil Nadu N=25	13	52.0	12	48.0
Andhra Pradesh N=25	10	40.0	15	60.0
Kerala N=20	13	65.0	7	35.0
Total N=120	57	47.5	63	52.5

(Contd.)

Protection of Civil Rights Act				SC/ST Abolition of Atrocities Act			
Aware		Not Aware		Aware		Not Aware	
N	%	N	%	N	%	N	%
6	7	8	9	10	11	12	13
39	78.0	11	22.0	19	38.0	31	62.0
19	76.0	6	24.0	7	28.0	18	72.0
18	72.0	7	28.0	6	24.0	19	76.0
15	75.0	5	25.0	7	35.0	13	65.0
91	75.8	29	24.2	39	32.5	81	67.5

Further, these respondents were not sure whether the laws were made by Parliament or State Legislatures.

There was relatively better awareness among the Brahmin and Christian police officers. The Non-Brahmin upper castes, were relatively poorer than the Brahmins. Even in personal interviews held with these police officers, the situation was rather identical.

Reasons for Different Laws

There is a lot of confusion and mis-understanding about the three legislations. Whether all the three legislations exist simultaneously and why different laws are needed are generally not understood. Whether the police is aware of the reasons for this was tested. The data are presented in table 4.2.

In general 55.8% police are not aware of the reasons for the different ligislations. In all the four states also the position is more or less similar. The highest degree of ignorance is found in Karnataka with 60% not knowing the reasons. Even in Kerala half of the police respondents do not know.

Among those who are aware for the different legislations, those who have full knowledge are extremely limited with just 9%. State-wise position is also similar excepting the small variation in the percentages. Those who know mostly come next with 14% in general. Karnataka accounts for the lowest percentage of 12. Those who have partial knowledge are around 21% in general and among all the States, Kerala has the best position with 25%.

In group discussions it was brought to light that the vast majority of the police think that Untouchability Offences Act is still in existence besides the PCR Act. Atrocities Act is just about three years old and hence its existence is still not widely known. But the basic reasons for enacting the Atrocities Act in the face of the PCR Act should have been known to the

TABLE 4.2

Knowledge of Reasons for enacting the different Laws

States	Fully Known N	Fully Known %	Mostly Known N	Mostly Known %	Partly Known N	Partly Known %	Not Known N	Not Known %
Karnataka N=50	4	8.0	6	12.0	10	20.0	30	60.0
Tamil Nadu N=25	3	12.0	4	16.0	5	20.0	13	52.0
Andhra Pradesh N=25	2	8.0	4	16.0	5	20.0	14	56.0
Kerala N=20	2	10.0	3	15.0	2	25.0	10	50.0
Total N=120	11	9.2	17	14.2	25	20.8	67	55.8

enforcing authorities. But the actual situation was quite different. Most of them started blinking when asked to say why it is called Protection of Civil Rights Act and why it was enacted when there was Untouchability Offences Act.

Sources of Information

Since the present study is confined to the PCR Act, the investigation mostly relates to this Act. Sources of information so far as the police are concerned are therefore in relation to the PCR Act. The data are presented in table 4.3.

Four sources are given by the police. These are literature on PCR Act, Orientation Courses for the police both in the form of training classes and refresher classes, officers telling their lower rank officers and news papers. In general, Orientation Courses have the best effect since 67% police respondents have quoted this. Among the different states also the position is more or less similar. While Karnataka accounts for 61.5% which is the lowest, Kerala has the highest percentage of 80. Tamil Nadu and Andhra Pradesh come in between.

Officers of higher ranking account for the next best source of information. Fifty-nine percent of the police respondents quote this source in general. State-wise, Kerala has the highest percentage of 80 and Karnataka has the lowest with 48.7%. Andhra Pradesh and Tamil Nadu are a little above 60%.

News paper accounts for 53.8% in general. Kerala stands highest with 86.7% and Karnataka lowest with 35.9%. Andhra Pradesh and Tamil nadu are in between. But Tamil Nadu is better than Andhra with 63%.

Literature meaning the full text of the Act as well as condensed version has the lowest percentage in general with 30.7%. While Kerala accounts for 60%, Karnataka has the lowest percentage of 12.8. Tamil Nadu is better than Andhra with 42%.

TABLE 4.3

Sources of information about the PCR Act among the police respondents

States	Literature		Orientation Courses		Officers		News Papers	
	N	%	N	%	N	%	N	%
Karnataka N=39	5	12.8	24	61.5	19	48.7	14	35.9
Tamil Nadu N=19	8	42.1	13	68.4	12	63.2	12	63.2
Andhra Pradesh N=18	6	33.3	12	66.7	11	61.1	10	55.6
Kerala N=15	9	60.0	12	80.0	12	80.0	13	86.7
Total N=91	28	30.7	61	67.0	54	59.3	49	53.8

Knowledge of PCR Act

Knowledge of PCR Act is what concerns most in the present study. It is pointed out in the earlier table that 91 out of 120 police respondents are aware of the PCR Act. And now an attempt is made to know the extent of knowledge about PCR Act possessed by the police. This information is coming forth in table 4.4.

The general position is that those who have a full knowledge of this law constitute nearly 11%. State-wise Kerala has the best position with 20% and Karnataka worst with nearly 8%. Tamil Nadu and Andhra are on par with 11%.

'Mostly knowledgeable' policeman are to the extent of 33% in general. While Kerala accounts for the highest percentage with 47, Andhra Pradesh has the lowest with 28%. Partly knowledgeable police account for the highest percentage in general (56%). While Karnataka and Andhra have the highest percentage of 61, Tamil Nadu has 58% and Kerala 33%.

Further insights were obtained during personal interviews and group discussions. A few questions were put to the groups for participation. Some of these are : Why the present law is called Protection of Civil Rights Act ? The group remained almost silent. The difference between the Untouchability Offences and Civil Rights were not known. What is Untochability and whether it has been defined under the Constitution or the Act ? There was no answer among the constables. Even a large number of Sub-Inspectors could not answer this. Whether the cases before the court could be compounded ? The general answer was positive. Can the police effect compromise when the victims bring the complaints to the police station ? The general understanding was affirmative. 'Why not, Sir. Is is not our duty to see that peace and harmony are ensured in the village ? If the victims themselves are for a compromise the police should accept this". This is the type of thinking that prevails among the police.

TABLE 4.4

Extent of the knowledge of the police about PCR Act

States	Fully Knowledgeable		Mostly Knowledgeable		Partly Knowledgeable		Total	
	N	%	N	%	N	%	N	%
Karnataka	3	7.7	12	30.8	24	61.5	39	100.0
Tamil Nadu	2	10.6	6	31.4	11	58.0	19	100.0
Andhra Pradesh	2	11.1	5	27.8	11	61.1	18	100.0
Kerala	3	20.0	7	46.7	5	33.3	15	100.0
Total	10	10.9	30	33.0	51	56.1	91	100.0

A clean distinction between cognizable and non-congnizable offences could not be made by the constables. However, a vast majority of the Sub-Inspectors could do this. The concepts of collective fine, summary trial, mobile courts and special courts were not known to the constables and head constables. Section 15 A is a very significant addition made. But this is not known to a vast majority of the police.

When asked as to why the PCR Act was enacted, who headed the Parliamentary Committee and when this law was made, non of them were able to answer. A few, of course, could give a faint idea. But their general ignorance was apparent.

Atrocities Act

Though the present study has nothing to do with the Atrocities Act, a few questions were raised with the respondents because there is definitely a linkage between the PCR Act and Atrocities Act. The police is expected to be familiar with the provisions of this law as well. The extent of knowledge possessed by the police is tested with the help of data in table 4.5.

As seen in the earlier table, only 39 police respondents are aware of this law. Out of them only one person is having the full knowledge and 5 persons (12.8%) having knowledge of a major portion of the law. State wise position is that the only person who has the full knowledge is from Kerala and 2 from Tamil Nadu and 3 from Kerala have known most of the law. Karnataka and Andhra Pradesh draw blank.

Partial knowledge is possessed by 84.7% police in general. State-wise, while Karnataka and Andhra have 100% in this category Tamil Nadu has 71% and Kerala 43%. This is because of the fact that Tamil Nadu and Kerala are generally more knowledgeable as pointed out earlier.

The distinction between the Civil Rights and Atrocities could not be established by a vast majority of the police. They could

TABLE 4.5

Extent of the knowledge of the police about the SC/ST Atrocities Act

States	*Fully Knowledgeable*		*Mostly knowledgeable*		*Partly Knowledgeable*		*Total*	
	N	*%*	*N*	*%*	*N*	*%*	*N*	*%*
Karnataka	—	—	—	—	19	100.0	19	100.0
Tamil Nadu	—	—	2	28.6	5	71.4	7	100.0
Andhra Pradesh	—	—	—	—	6	100.0	6	100.0
Kerala	1	14.2	3	42.9	3	42.9	7	100.0
Total	1	2.5	5	12.8	33	84.7	39	100.0

not explain the circumstances that led to the Atrocities Act. When stressed, some policemen said "Sir, the government is bringing out so many laws, so frequently, how do you expect us to know. Even the law makers may not remember. We do whatever our higher officers want us to do.

Source of Information About Offences

Police would act when the offence committed is communicated to it. The first source of information is very inportant. This issue was discussed with the police respondents. Table 4.6 deals with this.

It is seen from the table that the victims of the offence account for the best source. A little more than 47% of the first source of information comes from the victims themselves. There is not much difference among the various states so far as the first source is concerned, excepting that the percentages vary from State to State. While Kerala accounts for the highest percentage (55%) Karnataka has the lowest with the 42%. Andhra Pradesh is slightly better than Tamil Nadu.

The next source is Voluntary Organizations with 17% in general. While Kerala draws a blank here, the remaining states account for 20% each. Village poeple are a better source to the police than the voluntary organizations. In general 36% of the information comes from them. While Kerala accounts for the highest percentage (45%), Andhra Pradesh has the lowest percentage (28%).

Suggestions for Effective Implementation

Police is, as said earlier, generally held responsible for ineffective implementation of the Act. This type of feeling was expressed by a large number of respondents in the present study. But what version the police gives in defence even admitting that the police has not done its best. This sociological orientation to the problem is very important and relevant.

TABLE 4.6

First Source of information to the police about the offence

States	*Victims*		*Voluntary organizations*		*Village people*		*Total*	
	N	%	*N*	%	*N*	%	*N*	%
Karnataka	21	42.0	10	20.0	19	38.0	50	100.0
Tamil Nadu	12	48.0	5	20.0	8	32.0	25	100.0
Andhra Pradesh	13	52.0	5	20.0	7	28.0	25	100.0
Kerala	11	52.0	—	—	9	45.0	20	100.0
Total	57	47.5	20	16.7	43	35.8	120	100.0

The suggestions offered by the police respondents for effective implementation of the Act are contained in table 4.7. Four suggestions are offered by them. These are : More staff, Vehicle Travelling allowances and dearness allowances and rewards. The respondents have offered multiple suggestions.

The demand for more staff is made by 81% respondents in general. State-wise speaking, 90% police of Kerala has said so. Karnataka police accounts for the lowest percentage of 76. Tamil Nadu and Andhra Pradesh are in between. The contention of the police is that there is a steady increase in the number of incidences compared to the past. Police has to attend to several types of offences. New legislations are brought into force quite often and the existing police has to bear the responsibility of implementing the provisions of law. This is not possible until there is more police force.

Transport seems to be another acute problem from which police suffer. Even if they want to act swiftly, they are handicapped because of vehicle problem. A little more than 77% police say so in general. State-wise, Tamil Nadu and Andhra Pradesh account for the highest percentage of 84. Next comes Kerala with 80% and the last is Karnataka with 70%.

Payment of adequate travelling and daily allowances is another suggestion made by 70% policemen in general. Their contention is that what is paid to them now is totally inadequate when they have to visit big cities and stay there. They can-not pay from their pockets the extra money needed. They also felt that they can-not tax the victims for this purpose.

The opinion is more or less uniformly shared by a vast majority of the respondents of other states. While 70 and a little above percentage of respondents of Karnataka, Andhra Pradesh and Kerala offer this suggestion, 64% respondents of Tamil Nadu share this.

TABLE 4.7

Suggetions of the Police for effective implemenation of the Act

States	*More Staff*		*Vehicle*		*TA/DA*		*Rewards*	
	N	*%*	*N*	*%*	*N*	*%*	*N*	*%*
Karnataka N=50	38	76.0	35	70.0	36	72.0	15	30.0
Tamil Nadu N=25	20	80.0	21	84.0	16	64.0	12	48.0
Andhra Pradesh N=25	21	84.0	21	84.0	18	72.0	10	40.0
Kerala N=20	18	90.0	16	80.0	14	70.0	12	60.0
Total N=120	97	81.0	93	77.5	84	70.0	49	40.8

Forty one percent respondents in general suggested that suitable rewards would be a motivating factor. While 60% respondents of Kerala said so, the least are from Karnataka (30%). Tamil Nadu and Andhra Pradesh respondents account for 48% and 40%.

In group discussion policemen furthea elaborated this concept of reward. Reward, according to them is both recognition of the good work done and also are encouraging factor. To most of them, working against the local caste-Hindus who are economically and politically dominant is not a small thing. 'Sir, we have to risk our lives and jobs by encountering the dominant groups. Our higher officers give us a slip sometimes under pressure or even otherwise. If we belong to lower castes and the higher officers are upper-castes, we are in real trouble. Therefore, reward, not necessarily in the form of money, is a most welcome action of the state'.

This discussion led to further probe. A few case-studies were undertaken. One of them is briefly reported here.

Self : Krishnappa, which caste do you belong ?

Krishnappa : Sir, I am a Scheduled Castes

Self : Since you are a constable, do you get support from your higher officers in your work ?

Krishnappa : Sir, it all depends upon the type of officer. Sometimes our own caste people let us down very badly because they want to be in the good books of the local elite and higher caste officers. Sometimes higher caste officers will appreciate our work. In general, Caste-Hindu Officers will not be happy with us.

Self : Who are these Caste-Hindu Officers showing appreciation to you ?

Krishnappa	:	They are generally Brahmin officers.
Self	:	What about Muslim and Christian officers ?
Krishnappa	:	They are always sympathetic and helpful.
Self	:	How do the unhappy caste-Hindu officers treat you later ?
Krishnappa	:	They catch us under some other pretext. Sir, you know that policemen can be caught for various reasons. We will be troubled. We will be transferred. Our families suffer.
Self	:	What about your expenses in taking the witness to the court ?
Krishnappa	:	Sir, it is very difficult to manage. If we take the witnesses of the caste-Hindus, we will be taken care of by them. But if we take the victims, we have to face problems. Why should we pay from our pocket, Sir, Should not the government take care of our minimum needs ? If we are honest, we pay penalty.

Problems Faced by the Police

Police are expected to discharge their duties under all circumstances. But very rarely their problems are identified and solved. This is applicable to police at lower level as well as at higher level. This is the popular view. Hence, a brief intervention was made to know from the policemen of different ranks about the problems they face in the process of implementation of the Act and other measures of the State.

Table 4.8 has data on the problems of the police. Four problems have been mentioned. These are: local pressure, pressure from higher officers, pressure from the politicians and the Scheduled Caste activists. Local pressure surface in the context of the traditional social structure. Nearly 56% of the police refer to this. The Scheduled Castes suffer both from the caste and class discrimination as well as exploitation. The higher

TABLE 4.8

Problems faced by the police

States	*Local Pressure*		*Pressure from Officers*		*Pressure from Politicians*		*Scheduled castes activists*	
	N	*%*	*N*	*%*	*N*	*%*	*N*	*%*
Karnataka N=50	29	58.0	21	42.0	36	72.0	30	60.0
Tamil Nadu N=25	10	40.0	14	56.0	11	44.0	20	80.0
Andhra Pradesh N=25	20	80.0	21	84.0	22	88.0	21	84.0
Kerala N=20	8	40.0	9	45.0	8	40.0	16	80.0
Total=120	67	55.8	65	54.2	77	64.2	87	72.5

caste Hindus view the desire of the Scheduled Castes to assert their legal as well as human rights as a calculated challenge to the traditionally established and well recognized superiority of the caste-Hindus, particularly the dominant Non-Brahmin upper castes.

Further, in a closed society where the status of a person is still decided on his occupation, class plays a significant role. The Scheduled Castes are generally farm-labourers, manual labourers and at best marginal farmers. They generally work under the caste-Hindus employees, who have a virtual control over their life and property.

Thus, local pressure on the police not to go against this traditional social order is sometimes so strong that even the committed police has to face problems of relations from the local feudal lords. In Andhra Pradesh 80% police respondents quote this problem. Caste and class system is still very rigid in Andhra Pradesh. The position in Kerala and Tamil Nadu is much better. Only 40% policemen refer to local pressure. Even Karnataka is better than Andhra Pradesh.

The next problem mentioned is the pressure from the officers. Fifty four policemen in general refer to this. Here according to the respondents, 'Officers' means both police as well as administrative officers. These Officers bring pressure on the lower rank policemen either because of caste or money consideration. Some of the respondents had no reservation to produce enough evidences to confirm their statements. Some respondents said, "Sir, if we are convinced that we will not be harmed under any circumstances, we will definitely bring out the truth as to how higher officers receive money from the Caste-Hindus and try to hush up the cases. Sir, they even go to the extent of threatening the witnesses."

State-wise position is that Andhra Pradesh again tops with 84% of the respondents referring to pressure from higher officers. Kerala and Karnataka account for a little more than

40%. But in Tamil Nadu 56% quote this problem. A further probe revealed that in Tamil Nadu there has been an organised attack against the Scheduled Castes by the backward castes like the Uanniyans and this has influenced some police officers too.

Politicians have their own culture and values. They act according to this. Politicians have proved in many cases that they are the bosses of the policemen. Even honest and efficient police officers have either to succumb to the dictates of the politicians or face the obvious consequences. This is the message got from the respondents in the study. Sixty four percent respondents say that politicians exercise pressure on them. Some-times they incur their wrath if asserted. In Andhra Pradesh this is to the extent of 88% Karnataka follows next with 72%, Tamil Nadu and Kerala are much better with 44% and 40% respectively.

Another problem faced by the police is the increasing intervention from the Scheduled Caste activists called by different names in different states. According to the police respondents, pressure from the activists in the highest with 72.5% in general. Policemen are divided about the role of the activists. While Muslim, Christian, Brahmin and Backward caste policemen do feel that the interventions of the activists is timely and inevitable, some of the policemen belonging to the non-Brahmin upper caste feel bad about the type of intervention.

Those who welcome intervention feel that this would help the police in many ways and would ultimately lead to reduction in violation of the PCR Act. But those who are not happy with this intervention feel that this intervention results in increased workload and court cases. According to them, the activists force the police to take up cases.

Infact, this problem is uniformly seen in all the states. Andhra Pradesh tops with 84% police respondents giving this reason. Tamil Nadu and Kerala come next with 80%. Karnataka has the lowest percentage of 60.

When asked whether the activists are unnecessarily creating problems to the police, a vast majority of the latter said that the activists were concerned about the problems of the Scheduled Castes and they seem to have no faith in any dialogue. Any delay on the part of the police in booking cases and proceeding further would be misunderstood by the activists.

However, a small section of the police feels that the activists outdo their duty and do not have patience. The activists would observe dharna or take out protest march, raising slogans against the police. In some places there would be direct confrontation between the police and the activists.

False Allegations

There is a feeling that the Scheduled Caste people resort to false complaints against the caste-Hindus and thus try to take undue advantage of the legal prescriptions. Do the police share this view ? This issue was raised with them. Their opinion is furnished in table 4.9.

It is observed that a vast majority of nearly 82% respondents in general do not agree with the allegation that false complaints are lodged with the police. This is the opinion among the police in all the states. In Kerala 90% reject this allegation, whereas in the other three states 80% reject.

However, 18% of the police do say that there are false complaints. Nearly 7% say that most of the cases brought to the station are false and the rest say that sometimes false complaints are lodged. So far as the four states are concerned, while in Kerala none says that most of the complaints are false, in the other States 8% of them say that there are mostly false complaints. But so far as false complaints being lodged sometimes, there are around 10% in each State sharing this view.

TABLE 4.9

Opinion about false allegations

States	*Mostly false cases*		*Sometimes false cases*		*No false complaints*		*Total*	
	N	%	*N*	%	*N*	%	*N*	%
Karnataka	4	8.0	6	12.0	40	80.0	50	100.0
Tamil Nadu	2	8.0	3	12.0	20	80.0	25	100.0
Andhra Pradesh	2	8.0	3	12.0	20	80.0	25	100.0
Kerala	—	—	2	10.0	18	90.0	20	100.0
Total	8	6.7	14	11.7	98	81.6	120	100.0

The police were asked to give their reasons for bringing false complaints. They give four reasons for this. First, some of the bad elements among the Scheduled Castes develop hatred for their masters or creditors and take advantage of the law. Secondly, some Scheduled Castes are set up by the vested interest against them. Thirdly, political party leaders try to play mischief by provoking the Scheduled Castes. Fourthly, some Scheduled Castes people want to create an atmosphere of fear and tension in the villages for their own advantage.

However, a vast majority of the police did not agree with this. The main reason for this difference is due to caste factor. Only such of the police who had staunch attachment to their caste could give this type of expression. Muslim, Christian and the backward caste police did not share this. Even the Brahmins did not agree.

False Caste Certificate

It is generally said that some of the caste Hindus have misappropriated the benefits meant exclusively for the Scheduled Castes by producing false caste certificates. There are some names of the Scheduled Castes which can be slightly twisted and bring under the Scheduled Caste list. It is very easy to obtain such certificates in the taluk office. The CRE Cell is expected to deal with such cases too.

The police respondents were approched to indicate their views on this issue. Table 4.10 has relevant data. It is seen that in general, 30% police do agree that the allegation is true. Karnataka tops with 42% and the least is in Kerala with 10%. Tamil Nadu and Andhra Pradesh account for 28% and 24% respectively.

It is only in Karnataka that there is a strong feeling about false caste certificates. The CRE cell has also admitted this and more than 900 complaints are pending. What the police say is

TABLE 4.10

Production of false caste certificates-police point of view

States	*Agree*		*Do not Agree*		*Do not know*		*Total*	
	N	*%*	*N*	*%*	*N*	*%*	*N*	*%*
Karnataka	21	42.0	20	40.0	9	18.0	50	100.0
Tamil Nadu	7	28.0	13	52.0	5	20.0	25	100.0
Andhra Pradesh	6	24.0	14	56.0	5	20.0	25	100.0
Kerala	2	10.0	14	70.0	4	20.0	20	100.0
Total	36	30.0	61	50.8	23	19.2	120	100.0

that the government itself does not want any action to be taken against those who have produced false caste certificates.

Police in Andhra Pradesh and Tamil Nadu do have something to say about this issue. But they are not clear in their mind. In Kerala there is no such thing. But they know that such a thing prevails in Karnataka and therefore their answer pertains to Karnataka situation only.

What the police generally feel is that the government should not allow the benefits of the Scheduled Castes to be misappropriated by others. Strict action should be initiated. Some policemen said, 'Sir, if we are asked to proceed further and produce the list of such offenders, we will do a great service to the society. But do you think that the government will do this ? No one bothers about harm to the deserving ones'.

Nearly 51% police flatly reject the allegation. State-wise position is that in Karnataka 40% and in Kerala 70% reject this. A little more than 50% of the policemen in Tamil Nadu and Andhra Pradesh reject the allegation. But it is not that they do not believe at all. Their contention is that such a thing could never happen even if some-one wants to get a false caste certificate. Anyway, 19% remain neutral as they have not heard of this allegation at all.

About CRE Cell

Civil Rights Enforcement Cell is a body, as already explained earlier, entrusted with the task of ensuring effective implementation of the PCR Act. But the general understanding among many cross-sections of the knowledgeable population is that CRE is an extremely ineffective body. What opinion the police has about this ? Now many of them have heard of this ?

There was none among the police who had no knowledge of this Cell. There was unanimity among them about the ineffective functioning of the Cell. Some of the police had personal experience and some had learnt about this. When asked for the reasons, several reasons were advanced. There were multiple reasons furnished by each policemen. These reasons are presented in table 4.11.

There are four reasons advanced by them. These are : inadequate staff, uncommitted staff, pressure from above and frequent transfers. Eighty four percent police respondents in general feel that the CRE cell is not adequately staffed. Sometimes it had Deputy Superintendents and later on Superintendents of Police incharge. Sometime afterwards D.I.G's and I.G.P's were posted. By creating higher ranks the government cannot solve the problem, according to the police. What is required is the main office should have more staff and at the district and taluk level also more policemen should work for the Cell.

This opinion is common to all the Sates. While in Kerala 90% respondents hold inadequate staff as one of the reasons, even in other States 80 to 88% share this view.

The next reasons that the staff is uncommitted as advanced by 77% respondents in general. A vast majority of the respondents in all the States also hold this view. They say that all types of police personal are posted to the Cell. Some of them are even anti-Scheduled Castes. Some have no interest at all. Such indifferent and unconcerned police cannot do any good, according to the respondents.

Another reason that pressure is exercised from above is shared by 70% respondents in general and 70% to 84% in other States. While Tamil Nadu accounts for the highest percentage, Karnataka has the lowest with 70%.

Seventy seven percent police say that frequent transfers of the top officers incharge of the Cell harm the cell. There are

TABLE 4.11

Reasons for ineffective functioning of CRE Cell, according to the Police

States	*Inadequate Staff*		*Uncommitted Staff*		*Pressure from above*		*Frequent transfers*	
	N	*%*	*N*	*%*	*N*	*%*	*N*	*%*
Karnataka N=50	40	80.0	35	70.0	40	80.0	41	82.0
Tamil Nadu N=25	22	88.0	21	84.0	10	40.0	18	72.0
Andhra Pradesh N=25	21	84.0	20	80.0	20	80.0	20	80.0
Kerala N=20	18	90.0	16	80.0	14	70.0	14	70.0
Total N=120	101	84.2	92	76.7	84	70.0	93	77.5

instances, according to them, that within a few months the top officers have been transferred. The lowest percentage of 70 is in Kerala and the highest (82%) is in Karnataka.

Suggestions for Knowledge of Law

One of the deficiencies of the system is that the enforcing authorities have either limited or no knowledge of the legal prescriptions. Police respondents frankly admit this. They do have a desire to know more and more about the relevant legislations. They are not happy with the present system. Therefore, when asked for suggestions, they could offer five realy meaningful ones which are presented in table 4.12.

Nearly 82% of the police in general suggest that there should be regular classes for some -time to enable the police learn more and more about the legislations and the measures of the State. While 90% Kerala police suggest this, 78% Karnataka police say so. In between are Tamil Nadu and Andhra Pradesh.

The need for short summary of the Law was suggested by 86% respondents in general. These policemen want brief outlines on highlights of the Law in many languages easily understood by them. While 95% respondents in Kerala say so, in other States the percentage ranges between 82 and 88.

Seminars were suggested by 79% police respondents in general. While Andhra Pradesh tops with 92%, Karnataka has the lowest with 64%. Kerala accounts for 90% and Tamil Nadu for 88%. Seminars, the policemen say, should be easy and be given in small groups so that good discussions could be held.

Ninety six respondents suggest that the knowledge of law should be made compulsory as otherwise there will be no interest in learning. While in Kerala 100% respondents say so, in other States also 92 to 96% respondents do feel the need for compulsion.

TABLE 4.12

Suggestions for making the police know fully about the provisions of law

States	*Regular classes*		*Short summary of the Law*		*Seminars*		*Knowledge compulsory*		*Periodical tests*	
	N	%	*N*	%	*N*	%	*N*	%	*N*	%
Karnataka N=50	39	78.0	41	82.0	32	64 0	48	96.0	35	70.0
Tamil Nadu N=25	20	80.0	21	84.0	22	88.0	24	96.0	21	84.0
Andhra Pradesh N=25	21	84.0	22	88.0	23	92.0	23	92.0	20	80.0
Kerala N=20	18	90.0	19	95.0	18	90.0	20	100.0	18	90.0
Total N=120	98	81.7	103	85.8	95	79.2	115	95.8	94	78.3

Periodical tests should be held according to 78% respondents in general and a vast majority in all the States. While Kerala has the highest percentage of 90, Karnataka has the lowest percentage. There is a strong feeling that periodical tests should be held and this should be taken to assess the suitability of the police for further promotions and incentives.

CHAPTER V

Lawyers, Judges and PCR Act

As pointed out in brief in the Introductory Chapter, lawyers and judges have also a big role to play in effective implementation of the PCR Act. There are strong critics who hold the public-prosecutors and the judges responsible for the poor and slow implementation of the Act. Therefore, the views of the lawyers and judges were obtained and are now presented in this Chapter for discussion. The various issues discussed with the lawyers are :

1. General opinion of lawyers on certain issues,
2. Opinion of the lawyers about the role of Police,
3. Opinion about public-prosecutors,
4. Opinion about special measures for effective implementation of the Act
5. Opinion about problems of witnesses,
6. Opinion about training/orientation
7. Opinion about judiciary in relation to PCR Act,
8. Suggestions for clearance of arrears of PCR cases.

In limited discussions with a few judges and others, their opinion was obtained on the role of courts, problems of the courts and suggestions for improvements.

Opinion of Lawyers on General Issues

Lawyer respondents were asked to comment on four issues, namely present judiciary, CRE Cell, present Police strength and public prosecutors. Table 5.1 deals with this. When asked about adequacy or otherwise of the present judiciary, it is seen that half of the respondents say that it is adequate. Those who say that it is not adequate account for about one-third. A small percentage say that they cannot say anything definite.

So far as CRE Cell is concerned, 62% are of the opinion that the cell is not adequate to deal with the situation. A little less than one-third say that it is adequate. Some are neutral. A large number of the respondents constituting 75% say that the present police strength is inadequate. They are of the view that in the context of increased cases of violence, the existing strength is not adequate. A still higher percentage (81%) is of the opinion that the public prosecutors are not at all adequate.

About the Police

A few statements were placed before the Police for their comments, as presented in Table 5.2. About 65% respondents are of the opinion that the Police is not sincere in their duties. Those who support are around one-fourth. Lawyers say that if the Police is sincere, more cases could be traced and quick action be initiated.

Those who say that Police is ineffective constitute 65%. One-fourth do not agree, meaning thereby, that the Police is effective. Sixty nine per cent lawyers say that the Police will be under pressure and hence cannot deliver goods. A large

TABLE 5.1

Opinion of the Lawyers on certain issues dealing with the PCR Act

Opinion Issues	*Adequate*		*Not Adequate*		*Neutral*		*Total*	
	N	*%*	*N*	*%*	*N*	*%*	*N*	*%*
Present judiciary	26	50.0	18	34.6	8	15.4	52	100.0
Present CRE Cell	16	30.7	32	61.6	4	7.7	52	100.0
Present police strength	11	21.1	38	73.1	3	5.8	52	100.0
Present Public prosecutors	6	11.5	42	80.8	4	7.7	52	100.0

TABLE 5.2

Opinion of Lawyers about the role of police

Opinion Statement	*Agree*		*Do not Agree*		*Do not tknow*		*Total*	
	N	*%*	*N*	*%*	*N*	*%*	*N*	*%*
Police is sincere	14	26.9	34	65.4	4	7.7	52	100.0
Police is ineffective	34	65.4	14	26.9	4	7.7	52	100.0
Police is under pressure	36	69.2	8	15.4	8	15.4	52	100.0
Police is not sufficiently trained	40	76.9	10	19.2	2	3.9	52	100.0

number constituting 77% say that the Police is not sufficiently trained. Those who differ form this are extremely marginal.

About Public Prosecutors

Public prosecutors have a big role to play in trial and disposal of the cases. Table 5.3 has relevant opinion of the lawyers on this issue. Nearly 58% respondents say that the public prosecutors are not effective. About one-third differ from this view. Sixty nine per cent respondents say that separate public prosecutors are needed to deal with the PCR cases. Seventy seven per cent feel that the prosecutors should be accountable to the CRE Cell and be under the control of CRE Cell chief.

About Witnesses

Views of the lawyers were obtained on the problems of witnesses who form the backbone of the trial system. Table 5.4 deals with the problems of witnesses. Four statements were administered to the lawyer-respondents about the witnesses. These are : 'witnesses are under threat', 'witnesses are put to difficulties', 'witnesses lose income', and 'witnesses can be bought'.

A majority of the lawyers do admit that the witnesses are under threat (58%). Two reasons were advanced by them. First, most of the witnesses are Scheduled caste or Backward caste. The caste Hindus hold out threats in many ways and they can do whatever they feel like in village situations where caste-domination is still a powerful factor to decide the fate of certain groups. Secondly, these witnesses are often the employees or debtors of the dominant higher classes like landlords. Their very survival depends upon the good will of these people. Hence, who can dare the wrath of the higher caste and higher class groups. This is how the lawyer-respondents tried to explain the social phenomenon.

TABLE 5.3

Opinion about Public Prosecutors

Opinion Statement	*Agree*		*Do not Agree*		*Neutral*		*Total*	
	N	%	*N*	%	*N*	%	*N*	%
Public Prosecutors are effective	19	36.5	30	57.7	3	5.8	52	100.0
Separate Public Prosecutors	36	69.2	14	26.9	2	3.9	52	100.0
Public prosecutors should be under CRE Cell's control	40	76.9	10	19.2	2	3.9	52	100.0

TABLE 5.4

Opinion about problems of witnesses

Opinion Statement	*Agrce*		*Do not Agree*		*Neutral*		*Total*	
	N	%	*N*	%	*N*	%	*N*	%
Witnesses are under threat	30	57.7	10	19.2	12	23.1	52	100.0
Witnesses are put to difficulties	42	80.8	8	15.4	2	3.8	52	100.0
Witnesses lose income	50	96.2	—	—	2	3.8	52	100.0
Witnesses can be bought	36	69.2	16	30.8	—	—	52	100.0

The lawyers were also very clear and emphatic in their views that the consequences of giving evidence against the higher caste and class people would be disadvantageous to the witnesses. Eighty one per cent respondents share this view. These difficulties are apart from the threats. Drinking water would be stopped. Entry into hotels and temples would be made more difficult. Essential commodities might not be made available. Women-folk of the witnesses be troubled.

That witnesses would lose income was brought out by a vast majority of 96% respondents. These witnesses are poor. They are often manual labourers. They have to work hard and earn their daily income. If they have to go to distant places for giving evidence, they lose their income. What they get by way of compensation is not assured and timely, according to the lawyers.

Another important problem associated with the witnesses, according to 69% respondents is that witnesses can be bought by the accused. These witnesses, as said earlier, are poor. They do not always stand for values when they suffer from poverty. Any inducement would be adequate to win over them. This generally happens, according to the respondents, when the witnesses are from non-Scheduled caste groups. These witnesses either do not turn up before the court or will vitiate the merit of the case by giving different and conflicting evidences.

Special Measures

As discussed earlier, there are some special schemes or measures formulated by the government for effective implementation of the PCR Act. Some of these are : Need for mobile courts, special courts, summary trial, adequate financial support to the witnesses and Nyaya Panchayats at local level. The views of the lawyer-respondents are presented in Table 5.5.

The need for mobile courts is appreciated by the majority of the lawyers (69%). They feel that the Scheduled caste victims

TABLE 5.5

Opinion about special measures for effective implementation of PCR Act

Opinion Measures	*Agree*		*Do not Agree*		*Neutral*		*Total*	
	N	*%*	*N*	*%*	*N*	*%*	*N*	*%*
Mobile courts needed	36	69.2	10	19.2	6	11.6	52	100.0
Special courts needed	42	80.0	8	15.4	2	3.8	52	100.0
Summary trial needed	48	92.4	2	3.8	2	3.8	52	100.0
Witnesses to be financed adequately	50	96.2	2	3.8	—	—	52	100.0
Nyaya Panchayats at local level	28	53.8	18	34.6	6	11.6	52	100.0

and witnesses will be put to difficulties if they have to go to regular courts located at a distance. Secondly, this would consume lot of time. If the mobile courts are set up, it becomes easier for them to get justice.

In group discussion, the lawyers said that the mobile courts would be more useful and effective if they move to the villages where the offences take place. Justice can be speeded up too, according to them. If the mobile courts are located elsewhere, the very purpose is defeated.

The need for special courts was felt by a much higher percentage of lawyers. Eighty one per cent of them do feel the need to set up special courts. The lawyers make a clear distinction between mobile courts and special courts. Special courts are needed to attend to the cases arising out of the PCR Act. The regular courts cannot do justice because of the deficiencies inherent in the structure and style of functioning of the regular courts. The lawyers feel that special courts should be set up in such districts where the incidences of crimes are more and regular.

To the question whether mobile courts and special courts could be combined into one system, there was a consensus among them that it could be done and would serve the purpose better. Some of them said that this has been tried in some states.

Summary trial is welcome by 92% respondents. Lawyers do admit that the present elaborate and cumbersome system of trial is not helpful to the people. Consumption of time is too much. Procedures are too many. Quite often cases are adjourned for trivial reasons. People get disgusted. They lose faith in the judiciary. Therefore, it is better that the entire system of trial is re-examined and made simple. This is how the lawyers react to the concept of summary trial.

Lawyers do admit by a vast majority of 96% that witnesses should be adequately compensated for their loss of income. Some lawyers said, why should these people bother themselves by undergoing losses. It is the responsibility of the State to induce the witnesses to attend the courts regularly and help the prosecution and the victims.

Another measure which the lawyers suggest is to revive the traditional system of 'Panchayats'. Fifty four per cent of the respondents make this reference. The advantages are : cases are settled locally, lot of expenditure can be saved, people will be more bound by the decisions of the village elders. The question of appeal may not arise.

Of course, lawyers made it also very clear that the caste-bound village social structure might not allow this justice through panchayats so easily. But it would be worth making an attempt.

About Judiciary

As discussed elsewhere, judiciary is under attack for the ineffective implementation of the PCR Act. Opinion differs from group to group. A little later in this Chapter, views of the judges on this issue are also presented. A large number of the activists also feel bad about the judiciary. What do the lawyers say about the judiciary in relation to the PCR Act ?

As seen in Table 5.6, four statements were administered to the lawyers for their comments, namely adequacy of the present system, biased functioning of the judiciary indifference of the judiciary and heavy load of work in the courts.

Opinion of the lawyers is more or less evenly divided about the adequacy of the present system. Half of them agree with the statement that the present system is adequate. Sixtynine per cent do not agree with the view that the judiciary is biased. A vast majority of them also reject the view that the judiciary

TABLE 5.6

Opinion about judiciary in relation to PCR Act

Opinion Statement	Agree N	Agree %	Do not Agree N	Do not Agree %	Neutral N	Neutral %	Total N	Total %
Present system is adequate	26	50.0	22	42.3	4	7.7	52	100.0
Judiciary is biased	12	23.1	36	69.2	4	7.7	52	100.0
Judiciary is indifferent	10	19.2	38	73.1	4	7.7	52	100.0
Judiciary is over loaded	44	84.7	6	11.5	2	3.8	52	100.0

is indifferent. However, 85% of them do admit that the judiciary is overburdened.

Two significant results flow from this analysis. First, there is no unanimity on any of these issues. Secondly, lawyers are almost unanimous that if the courts have failed to deliver goods, it is virtually because of the fact that the courts are over-loaded.

Suggestions

In the previous table it is made amply evident that the main problem with the judiciary is that it is over-burdened. Hence disposal of PCR cases get delayed. Lawyers were able to offer some suggestions to overcome this problem. These suggestions are presented in Table 5.7. There are four suggestions made, namely additional judges should be appointed, there should be special clearance weeks, there should be redistribution of cases among the courts and definite period should be fixed for disposal of cases.

The majority of the lawyers (58%) feel that for a short period additional judges be appointed solely to dispose off the pending PCR cases as the present situation is not conducive. The lawyers feel that the judges cannot be solely held responsible. New legislations are on the increase and it becomes impossible for the judges to dispose off PCR cases which are also on the increase. Arrears should be cleared at any cost, according to the lawyers.

Another suggestion was that there could be some definite weeks designated for the purpose of clearance of the arrears (69%). This is also a temporary measure till the pending cases are cleared. Three-fourths of lawyers also say that if there are some courts overburdened and some courts with less burden, pending cases may be transferred to the latter courts. This does not involve any financial and procedural problems too, according to them.

TABLE 5.7

Suggestions for clearance of arrears of PCR cases

Suggestions	*Agree*		*Do not Agree*		*Neutral*		*Total*	
	N	*%*	*N*	*%*	*N*	*%*	*N*	*%*
Additional judges	30	57.7	18	34.6	4	7.7	52	100.0
Special clearance weeks	36	69.3	10	19.2	6	11.5	52	100.0
Distribute cases among less loaded courts	39	75.0	10	19.2	3	5.7	52	100.0
Deadline to be fixed	19	36.5	22	42.3	11	21.2	52	100.0

So far as 'dead line' to be fixed for the disposal of the cases is concerned, opinion is sharply divided. While 42% lawyers do not agree with the dead line issue, about 36% feel it is possible. Of course 21% remain neutral.

Those who opposed dead line argue that the disposal of the cases would depend upon several supporting factors. There is a link system. If something happens somewhere, the whole system gets affected. But they do admit that all possible steps are to be taken to clear the pending cases. Those who are in favour say that a reasonable time can be fixed so that wastage of time can be avoided.

About Orientation

The question of orientation or training has assumed greater significance and relevance today in many areas of activities. If the PCR Act is not effectively implemented and lack of knowledge and approach could be one of the reasons for this, orientation/training becomes useful. This issue was discussed with the lawyers. Their views are presented in Table 5.8.

Whether judges also should be given orientation ? Sixty nine per cent lawyers feel that this is needed. Refresher classes will help the judges particularly at the lower levels. There is nothing wrong in enabling the judges to attend such courses, according to the lawyers. They also said that a judge is always a student. Of course, there is adverse reaction by 27% lawyers. They feel that the judges study at home and why they should attend refresher courses.

That Police should be given orientation gets a lot of support from the lawyers. 92% of them hold this view. There is no opposition at all. Only a few remain silent. There lawyers say that Policemen are generally not in the habit of learning. Various legislations are enacted. Unless thy are made to understand these, they cannot effectively function. Orientation could be given periodically.

TABLE 5.8

Opinion about training/orientation etc.

Opinion Statement	*Needed*		*Not Needed*		*Netural*		*Total*	
	N	%	*N*	%	*N*	%	*N*	%
Judges should be given Orientation	36	69.3	14	26.9	2	3.8	52	100.0
Police should be given Orientation	48	92.3	—	—	4	7.7	52	100.0
Constant workshops should be held	50	96.2	—	—	2	3.8	52	100.0
Legal education through Literature	38	73.1	10	19.2	4	7.7	52	100.0

Ninety six per cent lawyers say that there should be constant workshops where lawyers, judges, police and CRE Cell along wits the social activists and researchers meet and discuss various issues objectively and ultimately help effective implementation of the Act. These workshops would enable the concerned officers readjust themselves.

Legal education through simple literature was suggested by 73% lawyers. They feel that simple booklets in different languages would enable all concerned understand the Law and the procedures.

Judges

The views of the judges were obtained on several issues relating to the effective implementation of the PCR Act. These issues are :

1. Role of the courts
2. Problems of the courts,
3. Suggestions for improvement.

The judges generally feel that the courts are doing their best to provide justice to the sufferers. They have no biases, prejudices or fear. Judges are also aware of the fact that quite often they are doubted and questioned "Either way, our judgements are not always well received. We are aware of this. After all we go by the facts of the case and evidence produced before the courts. If cases are not properly argued or if the first information reports are not properly prepared, what is it we can do ? You please remember that in our country motives are always attributed". This is how some judges reacted to the question "People generally lack confidence in the judiciary, Why ?"

Further dialogue with one judge provides greater insights

into the role of the judiciary. This is presented briefly as follows :

Director : Scheduled Castes people feel that the courts are biased in favour of the caste-Hindus. What do you say ?

Judge : I do not agree. Judges are there to provide justice.

Director : Do you mean to say that all the decisions are always fair ?

Judge : Yes. But what is fair is perhaps a relative term. The person who wins the case calls it fair and the person who loses generally calls it unfair. But people who have confidence in the judiciary take the judgement in the correct perspective.

Director : What about the caste factor in giving decisions ?

Judge : I do not endorse the view that caste factor decides the fate of the victim. Of course, I do not totally rule out some possible links through caste-factor. But a good judge is a God-fearing person and he does not bother about the caste factor.

Director : Why then are a large number of cases decided in favour of the caste-Hindus ?

Judge : There are many factors which shape the ultimate decision of the court. It all depends upon how well the Public prosecutor puts forth his arguments. It also depends upon the performance of the witnesses. Often the witnesses are tutored. They are induced. They are threatened. They become hostile witnesses.

On the other hand, witnesses of the defence are active, bold and clear in their evidence. This will make lot of difference.

Director : Are all judges well informed about the legal prescriptions ?

Judge : Well, a judge is always a student. He has to study hard and equip himself with the latest amendments. Hence, it is expected that the judges are well informed. But I do not rule out the possibility of some judges not being serious students of Law.

Director : Are there cases of compounding the cases ?

Judge : Not now. A few years ago there were instances of compounding the cases, This was done with the good intention of establishing harmonious relationship in the village and also out of ignorance of the latest Law not containing any provision for compouding.

Director : Is compounding of cases not against the interest of the Scheduled Castes.

Judge : Well, it could be. But compounding of cases will have positive results also. This cannot be totally ignored.

Director : How to make the judges fully equipped with the latest legal position ?

Judge : Well, as I said earlier, all judges are bound to be well equipped with legal position. But it is also good to have refresher courses for judges, particularly at the lower levels.

Director : Who should conduct these courses ? Can the administration do it ?

Judge : It is always better that the administration keeps away. I suggest that the Bar Council can arrange such refresher courses during vacations at different places, preferably at the district level.

Or alternatively the Judges Associations could also take up this issue. Government should liberally fund.

Director : What is your opinion on the present public prosecutors dealing with Civil Rights cases ?

Judge : Well, they are doing a good job. But their problems are :

1. They are too busy and

2. They have to depend upon the witnesses.

Director : Are the present courts adequately staffed to take up PCR cases and dispose them off early ?

Judge : No, the present courts are over-loaded. Our procedures are so complicated and cumbersome that it takes lot of time for disposal. Cases are adjourned for whimsical reasons. Lawyers do not co-operate properly. Witnesses are not produced on time. All these factors definitely affect the working of the courts.

Director : A very high percentage of cases are still pending. How to clear these cases ?

Judge : I appreciate this question. Accumulation of cases is bad. People loss faith. Justice delayed is justice denied. Some quick measures have to be initiated immediately. Additional judges have to be posted to such courts where the arrears are alarming. Arrears clearance week or month should be thought of.

Director : What is your opinion about mobile courts, special courts and summary trial ?

Judge : I welcome all these measures which give relief to the victims, witnesses and also to the regular courts. They are well thought of. But Government is slow in effective implementation.

Director : What is your opinion about CRE Cell ?

Judge : The Cell needs reinforcement and its branches to be located in all district headquarters.

Director : Do you favour Scheduled Castes judges to head the mobile and special courts ?

Judge : Not necessary. If Scheduled Caste judges are appointed, the caste-Hindus may give a different colour. Instead of caste factor, good and efficient judges could be appointed to give justice.

This particular case-study helped the research team to get into certain insights into the problems. When contacted the other judges too shared these views. It means that the judges do not find fault with the court for pendency of cases. But they are also aware of the deficiencies inherent in the overall system. By and large caste is not a force to be reckoned with in treating the cases under the PCR Act.

They are virtually unanimous in their views that it is the enforcement system that needs immediate attention. If the Police force is inadequate to meet the situation, what courts can do ? This is the trend of their arguments.

Judges were not prepared to comment on the politicians and political parties. They preferred to remain silent. Inspite of best efforts, they did not want to say anything about the politicians. Of course, they were co-operative in making suggestions to enable judiciary dispose off the cases as early as possible.

So far as the merits of PCR Act are concerned, they felt that the existing law is adequate if attempts are made sincerely to enforce it properly. About the witnesses, the judges feel that the poor people should be taken into confidence and th r expenses should be fully met by the State. Loss of income should also be adequately compensated. To the question whether the caste-Hindus should be made to meet the expenses, the judges felt it could be possible.

The judges have no reservations in expressing their views that refresher courses for judges at the lower level in particular should be held frequently. Various decisions of the coutrs on matters relating to PCR Act should be codified and the summary of this should be circulated among the judges too.

About the need for giving legal education to the people, there was no difference of opinion. They felt that if properly educated about legal provision, the people might realise the consequences. There was also almost unanimous opinion among them that there is no need to have further laws on this issue. It is sufficient if the existing PCR Act fully implemented. Too many legislations more or less on the same issue might not serve the purpose.

Case Studies

Five case-studies are presented here. These case studies throw lot of light on the working of the Police and the judiciary.

1. *Case-study of Mr. Gurulingappa*

Mr. Gurulingappa is an Advocate and Professor of Law. He is also involved in the activists movement. His views are : "Fortyfour years of independence have still left Hindu Society cold about the basic problem of Scheduled Castes, which is to restore to them the dignity that is theirs as free citizens of India. However, much we may try, we cannot eradicate what has been established by custom of thousands of years, and in support of which scriptures have been quoted or misquoted, as you know, even the devil can quote scriptures.

As it is well said that "He who has not suffered from the pain of sore feet cannot appreciate the feeling of pain in others". This maxim holds good in case of the Police in Karnataka. Their role in considering matters pertaining to the Weaker sections is very much diplorable. The moment the complaint is filed before the Police in respect of any social disability, the Police will not entertain and they will delay the proceedings by yielding to the highly influencial classes. Thereby they will not get justice from the Police side. Therefore in my opinion recruitment of the Police Department from among the Scheduled Castes and Scheduled Tribes at least to the extent of 40% or according to their population is very much necessary. In every Police Station atleast two Constables and One Assistant Sub-Inspector or Sub-Inspector belonging to the Scheduled Castes must be posted to entertain the grievances aired by the Scheduled Castes. If this is done every Villager belonging to Scheduled Castes will feel encouraged and it will be a moral booster for their community.

The Government has already appointed Civil Rights Enforcement Cell to take up the matters pertaining to the Scheduled Castes and Scheduled Tribes and they are doing their best to help this community, but the basic factor is that they are caught in the clutches of the communal forces. Even their genuine cases will be failed due to so many factors. But Hindu Society has yet to realise that true religion does not sanction untouchability. There are still serious aberrations here and there, and we get reports of ill-treatment of Scheduled Castes and Scheduled Tribes and physical violence done to them and attrocities on them. The Administration has come to appreciate that much remains to be done.

Therefore, let there be a reminder to every one that the old order cannot continue any longer, traditional prejudices and discriminations must end, and full opportunity must be given to Scheduled Castes for employment, for land ownership, and for other facilities that may raise their educational and economic level. I have talked of land ownership, because Scheduled Castes are generally the landless.

It is often said that an ancient wrong which has subsisted for centuries cannot be redressed all at once. But that makes it all the more necessary that those who are leaders of public opinion and those who are in authority see to it that fullest opportunity is provided to the members of the Scheduled Castes to rise to the level of others and that the benefits extended to them by the Government actually reach them.

The feeling of insecurity lingers on, strengthened, each time there is a communal orgy, many burnt alive, murdered, women folk were molested. Therefore, every Indian Dalith harbours this fear. It has hampered their full and bold participation to National Activity.

As flame communicates from coal to coal the caste system in India succeeds from generation to generation without any change, like total invalids they cling to the higher castes for their sustenances, survival and salvation and continue to live on the alms and mercies of the caste-Hindu rulers. They have become easy victims of envy, jealousy, injustice, harassment and humiliation.

In the circumstances, the Government must try to give top priority in the recruitment of Scheduled Castes and Scheduled Tribes in the Police Department, to safeguard the interests of Scheduled Castes and Scheduled Tribes in our State.

So far as judiciary is concerned, we need not stress more upon it for it is an independent and autonomous body. Only the reciprosity and reapproachment between the Government and the privileged people must be there to elevate this class from the disability which has been practiced by the higher caste-Hindu from time immemorial".

2. *The second case-study is that of Mr. Sridharan, presently an Advocate and an activist.*

"I shall start my essay with a quotation from Lord

Macaulay. In 1835 he said "It may be that the public mind of India may expand under our system till it has out grown that system; that by good Government we may educate our subjects into a capacity for better Government; that having become instructed in European knowledge they may, in some future age, demand European institutions. Whether such a day will ever come, I know not".

Such a day did dawn on 26th November 1949. On that fateful day the people of India solemnly resolved to constitute India into a Sovereign Democratic Republic and enacted and gave a constitution unto themselves for the purpose of securing to all its citizens justice, liberty, equality etc. Now after forty four long years, Dalits are asking where is that equality, where is that social and economic justice. When a Dalit attempted to drink coffee from a hotel like any other customer he was beaten to death. Forcing Dalits to eat night soil is becoming the order of the day. Why all these atrocities ? Because they are Dalits. As Shylock asked-Hath not a Dalit eyes, Hath not a Dalit hands, Hath not a Dalit senses, affections, passions ? Fed with the same food, subject to the same diseases heated and cooled by the same winter and summer as a caste Hindu is. If you prick us do we not bleed if you tickle us do we not laugh ? Then why this hostile discrimination towards Dalits ?

Now what are the Civil Rights ?. Mr. Justice G. K. Miller says, "It is difficult to give a comprehensive definition of Civil Rights. In my view they are not limited to common law right only and would include inter alia any right to property, reputation, status and office of a person though they may be-creatures of statutes". Thus securing civil rights to Dalits includes securing not only social justice but also economic justice.

What has been the role of intellectuals in securing justice to Dalits ? Almost all the intellectuals are of the opinion that their duty is only to interpret impassionately what the facts are. They discover life saving drugs. They also discover life destroying bombs. They say science is neutral towards values. What can we do with such intellectuals ? I have tried to involve some of them in social action but did not succeed. I had an occasion to meet some of the scavengers working in Manasa Gangotri, Mysore. They informed me that they would be evicted shortly from their houses. They took me to their area. There were about one hundred houses built on Government land. They had no authorisation. They were facing eviction. I convened a meeting of the residents. Many top intellectuals from Manasa Gangotri attended and addressed the meeting. Later it was resolved to submit a memorandum to the Deputy Commissioner praying to regularise the occupancy of those people. Four representatives from the area and the intellectuals were to start the next day at 3 PM from Manasa Gangotri to the Deputy Commissioner's Office. The next day when the delegation was to start no intellectual was seen at Manasa Gangotri at 3 PM. I along with the four representatives went to the Deputy Commissioner's Office. Sri Devanur Mahadeva was waiting for us at the D. C's Office. Others did not turn up. The Deputy Commissioner refused to receive our Memorandum.

Now coming to the role of legal luminaries, the position is not very encouraging. I include Hon'ble Judges also in the category of legal luminaries, because of the recent trends of Judicial activism. The legal profession is supposed to uphold the Constitution and the rule of law. Article 46 of the Constitution says "The State shall promote with special care the educational and economic interests of the weaker sections of the people, and in participation in particular of the Scheduled Castes and the Scheduled Tribes and shall protect them from social injustice and all forms of exploitation. Are not the Hon'ble Judges duty bound to uphold this part of the Constitution also ?

I would like to point out one instance to show how unconcerned and uncommitted, the legal luminaries in

Karnataka have been to the philosophy of social change for which the Constitution stands. There were village offices like THOTI, NEERGANTI etc., manned by the Scheduled Castes. A piece of land was attached to the Office and the holder of the Office was not paid any salary and he had to eke out his living by cultivating the land attached to the Office. The Karnataka Legislature abolished the village offices. The land attached to the office was to be regranted to the holder of the Office. In majority of cases the land had already been alienated unauthorisedly by the holder due to poverty. The intention of the Legislature was to give the land to the holder of the village office and not to recognise any right in the unauthorised holder whose position was not better than a tresspasser. But the Hon'ble High Court gave a ruling that the unauthorised holer cannot be evicted. The effect was what was taken away from the unauthorised holders by the legislature was conferred on them by the Court. The Thotis and Neeraguntis lost their lands. The legal luminaries are obstructing delivery of social and economic justice to Dalits.

Dalits, therefore, have no faith in the intellectuals and in the legal luminaries. They have therefore, decided to go it alone. They have started educating their masses. They are organising and agitating. They do not wait for any one to come and support them. They are leaving Mahatma Gandhi and his institutions. They are flocking around Dr. B.R. Ambedkar whom they consider as their massaih and emancipator.

An impression has gained ground among Dalits that the revenuc department is meant to help the landlords attempting to snatch away the land of Dalits; the Police is meant to protect the moneyed against the interests of Dalits, and the I.P.C. is enforced only against Dalits. Added to these comes the series of false criminal cases now being booked against the enlightened Dalit youths engaged in organising Dalits. The result is that Dalits feel physically and mentally isolated from the main stream of society. There is total alienation. 25% of the population feel that they are aliens in their own country. This is not a healthy trend. It has ominous signs. It protends danger to the unity and integrity of the nation.

This trend has to be reversed at any cost. The intellectuals have to come out of their seclusion. The lawyers should stand by the State when constitutional violence is used for delivering justice, social and economic to the weaker sections of the Community. There is an organisation called "the Peoples Council for social Justice "functioning in Kerala. It is patronised by legal luminarise like Mr. Justice V.R. Krishna Iyer (Retd), Smt. Justice Janaki Amma (Retd.) and others. It organises seminars and workshops for the education of the people on important welfare legislations. One such workshop was conducted at Ernakulam. It was inaugurated by Mr. Chief Justice Malimath and the function was Presided over by Sri Santhosh Hegde, Advocate General of Karnataka.

I do not subscribe to the view that there should be a mental change in the caste Hindus towards Daliths, and that the caste Hindus should change their attitudes. Expecting changes in the attitudes of caste Hindus is not a correct approach. We have to seek our remedies elsewhere. I feel that Daliths suffer because of their ignorance, not in the metaphysical sense in which the word ignorance is used in Philosophy, but in the empirical sense. What we need to do is to remove this ignorance and to give them education. What we can do in this regard is the crux of the problem. The remedy is compulsory education and Dalits themselves will do the rest".

3. *Case-study of Mr. Chandar*

Mr. Chander is an Advocate and an activist. His views also pertain to the Nature, extent and limitations of the Role of Police, district administration and judiciary. According to him "The Hindu Society is a diabolical body. The status of an individual is ascended or descended in the society in proportion to the ascendency and descendency of the caste status of an individual.

To overcome this despicable condition of the Scheduled Castes in the Society, the Constitution was framed with a prime object of creating equality as against the Anti-Human attitude of the past. The protection of Civil Rights Act is enacted to punish the offenders, who adopt, preach and practice untouchability against the principles of equality denouncing the said principles of equality by vowing allegiance to the superstitious theories based on caste and creed, agmas and dogmas.

Inspite of the pronouncement to the world outside that India is the secular country, the discrimination against individual in the name of caste is perpetuated. The fact remains that the atrocities on Scheduled Castes continue either with the connivance of local political leaders or with connivance of the Executive officials of the State who believe in statusquo to continue the present despicable social, political and economic order operating against the Scheduled Castes.

Now through this forum we must find out the remedial measures to controvert the impending evils against the Scheduled Castes through the Police, District Administration and Judiciary.

The Police is a formidable authority in the administration of Law and Order. The Police force is always drawn either from the ruling community or from the landed gentry, who always believe in statusquo.

To overcome this, a Special Police mostly drawn from the under privileged, should be formed with a conviction that the people who denounce the Constitutional rights are the real offenders against the country and the people who believe in caste ridden society are the enemies of the Nation.

In this perspection the Special Police be empowered to have the jurisdiction at Hobli, Taluk and District level to investigate the offences against the Scheduled Castes and Police must be properly rewarded for their good services and likewise punished severely for their negligence and partisan attitude by a supervisory body drawn from the members of under privileged class.

The Special Police must be headed by a special officer of the rank of an Inspector General of Police. The Special Police must be provided with Twentyfive per cent of the reserve of sources out of the total amount spent for the Police in the State. The twenty five per cent of our people are Scheduled Castes and under-privileged.

The Police must be empowered to put the collective fine summarily on the people in the defined area in a village who commit the atrocities against the Scheduled Castes, as in the case of Traffic offences. The said collective fine should be recovered as arrears of the land revenue by the State.

The Police must be ordained with the duty of giving protection to the spouse who marrys outside the caste. The offences such as rape-humiliation, assault, murder etc. against the Scheduled Castes should be detected within the specified period and the crimes which go undetected must be properly explained to the superior and the informant who furnishes information to the Police to detect the crime should be protected.

If there is any caste trouble in a specified area immediately the Government should declare that area as Protected Area. The persons who are held guilty of offences against the Scheduled Castes should be disqualified for contesting the election.

The next point is the role of District Administration. The Revenue Officers such as Tahsildars, Sub-Divisional Magistrate and the District Magistrates are forming a vital set up in the administration. They should consider the economic conditions of the Scheduled Castes in the areas when they prepare plan for their respective areas.

In the villages the lands which remain uncultivated must be distributed to the landless Scheduled Castes. Either the State or the Nationalised Banks should finance the Scheduled Castes for cultivating such lands distributed to them.

The Caste Certificates should be issued to the Scheduled Castes on the basis of report from the village Secretaries, on that basis, the Identity card with the photo countersigned by the Tahsildars should be given to carry till the end of the career of the concerned person.

The reservation in the allotment of shops in the market places and shandy should be made to the Scheduled Castes as compulsory. The needy Scheduled Castes persons should be assisted with necessary financial requirement either through Government agencies or through the Nationalised Banks.

The villages, which are devoid of caste atrocities should be adjudged as the Model village and suitable rewards should be given to such villages so as to encourage communal harmony.

Judiciary has an independent role in the interpretation of the Law. The judges make Law in their interpretation. The Kannada language was made the official language at all levels. Because a lot of Law Graduates are passing out from Universities every year, it is very easy to appoint the Scheduled Castes persons for the appointment of the lower judiciary and the Government must sincerely appoint the required reserve candidates in all the lower courts and no appointment of other candidate should be made till the eighteen per cent of the reservation is filled up.

The advocates from among the Scheduled Castes should be appointed to represent the cases of Nationalised Banks, Insurance companies, Government agencies and the quasi-Government agencies, so as to avoid the concentration of a few dominant communities in these areas of practice. This will stimulate the Scheduled Castes people to enter in as Legal Practitioners more and more and indirectly it will stimulate them into judiciary next.

It is wrongly believed that the reservations for the highest judiciary like High Courts and the Supreme Court are not necessary. When the Constitution has recognised reservations in special cadres like I.A.S., I.P.S. and I.F.S. the same formula should be applied to Judiciary also. It is evident to note that the judgements are ruled and over-ruled by the judges of Higher Judiciary. So the principle of no reservation of Higher Judiciary is anamoly of the Constitution. It is the word coined by the vested interests to shun the opportunity of the Scheduled Castes in the Highest Judiciary."

4. Case study of Mr. Aryamitra

Mr. Aryamitra is a retired IAS Officer with lot of judicial and administrative background, both as a District Magistrate and Collector. His views are :

"Various Constitutional provisions have been provided to achieve the objectives of the preamble. Special enactments like :

The Protection of Civil Rights Act 1985 and the Prevention of Social Disabilities Act 1955 have been on the Statute Book seeking the protection of Civil Rights of the weaker sections. Measures have also been provided for disqualification of members of the Parliament and State Legislature under the representation of the People's Act 1951. Thus, there are adequate and sufficient provisions made for the protection of these weaker sections.

Inspite of these, we are witnessing various crimes and atrocities like murder, rape, grevious hurt, arson in addition to various kinds of discrimination and disability inflicted on the so called 'Untouchables'.

In this process, the role of Police, District Administration and the Judiciary is paramount.

Police : Police has a special duty or obligation to enforce various provisions provided for safeguarding the rights and privileges of these people. The crimes are on the increaee. Disposal of cases pending with Police without investigation, submitting FIRs and Charge sheets are few. Police have to take up cases on their own. There is default in initiating enquiry. Action is not initiated even if the complaints are lodged. There should be sincerity and honesty in implementing these provisions. Often the complaints end in filing 'B' reports. Many a time, there is silence, helplessness, and disregard to the directions given to the Police. There is no prompt reporting on the action taken to the higher authorities. Cases are pending for undue long period. There is also interference on the police by the authorities in position and local leadership. Right type of people are not posted. There will be either too frequent changes or some will be retained unduly for a long period. Training and incentives are not adequate. New orientation and direction is necessary to the Police at the lower levels. Cases against "untouchables" require the most careful scrutiny and handling by an active and alert Police. There should not be unwarranted rejections on mere technical grounds in respect of grievances received. The powers of the Police should be certain and specific.

There should be impartial investigation of all complaints filed, there should be justification for rejection. The relation between the Police and Public should be cordial. The main task of the Police is to detect crime and catch the criminals. We are not living in a Police State but in a Welfare State. We have to look to the Police as friend, guide and philosopher. They are the guardians of the people afflicted with grievances.

Administration : The District Administrator is the leader in the District, a Coordinator, a pace setter and a Captain of the Ship. He sets up a standard and example to others in the District. He contributes and unifies all forces in the District for the balanced development of all activities for the welfare of the people. He is the positive instrument for implementing and executing all welfare measures. He identifies with the people. He always thinks of his district, his people. He fights for their interests. He is the servant of the people. He has a method in his working, has a right attitude to public. His relation with his Ministers and Politicians is percarious. He has to have a mental discipline. He has no compromise with Principles and Policies. He takes his colleagues with him. He represents them. He has no distrust, dislike or doubt with his co-workers. He is 'Primus inter pares'. He has to be democratic, public spirited, dedicated and patriotic. He is committed to his functions and duties.

"Maintenance of Law and order is like the riding of a horse. Once you (DM) let it get out of control, it bolts and recovery of control is a difficult process". The two (the S.P. and the D.M) have to work as parts, of one whole, the upper and the lower jaws as it were with the same wavelength, able to think with the same mind, with most complete confidence, mutual trust, respect and good faith. They should sink their differences and stand shoulder to shoulder to meet the challenges. They should not have tempermental differences.

Contrast with this, we have the period in the District most difficult, dull and dark. The responsibilities and duties look like divided and diverted. There is mutual distrust and dislike. The activities are not coordinated. There is no cooperation with the coming in of Zilla Parishads many think that the functions and duties of Deputy Commissioners are diluted, disjuncted and distributed. People no more think of him as the 'king pin' in the District. Government have to restate the policy regarding the prime responsibility of maintaining 'Law and order' and safeguarding the interests of weaker sections in the District. People have come to accept the administrative inefficiency as a tact of life and make allowances for it in every thing they do. People have become conscious, alert and mature. They have become allergic to authority and discipline. It has become difficult to contral. Deputy Commissioner has to enact a crucial role, doing all sorts of miscellaneous jobs. He is grumbling. His tasks are onerous, numerous and varied. Whenever Government wants a particular job to be done, it will be entrusted to the Deputy Commissioner. The test of a good officer lies in his capacity for keeping things in order and quiet. He has to cope up with all sorts of emergencies which are extra ordinary, delicate and complex.

Judiciary: It is expected of the judiciary to give a fair trial to the man seeking justice. Independent judiciary and procedural safeguad are essential to liberty. Law is not merely a matter of coercion and punishment, but it is its task to set standards of justice, acceptable to the society. There is dearth of case law in respect of administration of justice touching the civil liberties. There is lack of judicial review of administrative interferences with the enforcement of Civil liberties. There is no sympathetic interpretation of law. Law has to be seen as a positive instrument in the implementation of national policy. Judge is an umpire to avoid clashes, and should cut off from the conflicts and interests while safeguarding the rights and freedom of citizens. There is no proper judicious inquiry into many legal problems. Unfortunately, there is no Civil liberties movement. There is no vigorous campaign against many forms of oppression to preserve the liberty. Rights are granted but not protected. Their maintenance requires constant vigilance. People should become aware of their rights and be prepared to assert them as their basic right with self respect.

Offenders are to be deterred from committing offences, punishment should serve as an example to others. Criminals have to be deterred from defying the authorities of State and Majesty of the law.

"A country whose judiciary is weak or otherwise unsatisfactory and does not enjoy the full cofidence of the public, cannot hope to be a progressive or happy country".

I have given separately two case studies indicatlng how at every stage, there is failure and fault in safeguarding the interests of the Harijans".

Mr. Aryamitra has narrated two interesting instances of the justice done to Scheduled Castes.

I. A Harijan family of six were cultivating a sizeable extent of land for decades, in the outskirts of a Sub-Division Headquarters. The lands were fed by a major irrigation project. The land was adjoining the lands of a rich, influencial, dominant community leader holding village offlce position as Chairman. This Harijan family was subjected to frequent harassment, illtreatment, abuse, attempts to dispossess the peaceful enjoyment of land by this "hand Lord". The crops were often cut and removed at the behest of this Chairman. The Harijan had complained several times to all the Revenue. Police authorities for protection and to safeguard his interest over his lands. None had responded to give protection. The Assistant Commissioner of the Sub-Division had sent these complaints received to his Revenue Subordinates and Police for action.

Harassment continued unabated. No protection was given. One early morning, when the Harijan family was removing the weeds in their lands, the "Land Lords" henchmen brutally used violence with sickle and other weapons and caused grievous injuries on the bodies of six members of the Harijans. The local sympathisers of these victims rushed to the residence of the Assistant Commissioner to rescue these injured. Assistant Commissioner asked the Tahasildar and Inspector of Police of the town to render medical aid to these injured and take action against the offenders. At that time local J. M. F. C., Deputy Superintendent of Police were present. None of these offlcers moved to render their help, protection or aid to the injured. After noticing these happenings, Assistant Commissioner himself went to the lands, where the injured were lying and removed them to the hospital for treatment. The Doctor of this Government hospital also did not attend to these injured immediately. After considerable time waiting outside the hospital with the injured, Assistant Commissioner rushed to the chambers of the R.M.O. and asked him to attend to the injured immediately. Then also the doctor delayed. Assistant Commissioner has to be rough with the doctor. Thereafter the injured were attended to without special attention. These was huge crowd outside the Hospital premises and urged the Assistant Commissioner to take appropriate action.

The Deputy Commissioner and Superintendent of Police were away in Bangalore, on official duty. After three days of this incident, both of them rushed to the Sub-Division Headquarters to ascertain the details of the incident. Assistant Commissioner had already sent report to them. Assistant Commissioner was waiting for them. Deputy Commissioner accompanied by Assistant Commissioner took a detour covering 120 miles to ascertain the details from Assistant Commissioner. It was complained to the Deputy Commissioner by a section of the town against the Assistant Commissioner that he used force on the Doctor, and even assaulted him while removing the injured to the hospital. Stories were built up on the incident. Deputy Commissioner ascertained about the true facts from the Assistant Commissioner of the incident and was satisfied.

After a lapse of about a month, Superintendent of Police and Deputy Commissioner again visited the town and informed the Assistant Commissioner that he has to face the consequences of being an important witness for the prosecution and it was not a happy thing for an officer of Assistant Commissioner status to appear before the Court. Assistant Commissioner was called to be a witness after a year, from several places he was working. He was the first person on all occasions to be present in the Court. The Assistant Commissioner was not examined by the Court even though he was called upon to appear before the Court several times. The Public Prosecutor, Advocates were well known to the Assistant Commissioner. The trial of accused completed without the evidence of an important witness like the Assistant Commissioner, some of the other witnesses were stated to have turned hostile, as they were won over. It was learnt that the accused were let off. Out of the six injured, three died of the injuries.

II. A village 'N' had a population of about 1300, consisting of about 1000 belonging to a very rich dominant community and the rest Harijans. The major community members were land-lords owning wet lands raising atleast two cash crops. The Harijans were mostly agricultural labourers dedending upon mostly the wages as bonded labourers working in the houses of local rich people. The Hobli headquarters named 'B' was about 10 km from the village 'N'. There was a T.D.B. local hospital in 'N' village. The village 'B' is fairly a big one with all modern facilities like the Police Station with Sub-Inspector of Police, L.F. Dispensary and educational institutions. The Hobli headquarters 'B' was about 20 km from the District Headquarters.

It is said that a Tahsildar of the Taluk was tied to a tree by the rich influential people of village 'N' who had gone there to collect arrears of L.R. and other Government dues. This had happened about 20 years ago. Since then, no officer worth name had the courage to visit the village 'N'. This village had several rowdy elements. The poor were under the clutches of the rich. With the spread of education and financial stability, certain sections of the Harijans were refusing to serve as slaves in the fields of the rich. They became stubborn and refused to be bonded to the rich. The rich became restive and wanted to teach the Harijan family a lesson. There were atrocities committed on this family.

One day, the three members of this family were cut on their arms, legs, causing injuries. All the three injured were locked inside a small tiled roofed room and were set fire by rich. No body came to the rescue of this innocent family including the local officials. The other Harijans were afraid to render any assistance to the injured. This incident had happened early in the morning. None from the villages 'N' or 'B' or Taluk had come to the rescue of this torture. Some one from the village had informed the Deputy Commissioner about this attempt to murder. The Deputy Commissioner immediately rushed to the village all alone. It was about noon. The village 'N' looked deserted, most of the doors were shut. None came out, Deputy Commissioner took a round of the village, visited the Harijan colony and freed the injured. He took the 3 injured in his Car to the District major hospital for immediate treatment. Deputy Commissioner had taken photos of the injured, prior to the admission to the hospital.

Thereafter Deputy Commissioner went again to villages 'N' and 'B' and made enquiries on the incident. Deputy Commissioner kept under suspension the medical staff and Police Sub-Inspector at the village 'N' and 'B'. Visited the Office of the Sub-Inspector of Police and saw the records of complaints made by the Harijans of harassment and atrocities committed on them by the rich. No action had been taken on the complaints against the offenders, as they were all rich and influential. The news of the suspension of the P.S.I. had spread like wild fire without lapse of time. Deputy Commissioner himself had prepared the files against six of the important leaders of the major community and had passed detention orders under M.I.S.A. for harassment and atrocities on Harijans. Five out of 6 had been detained by Police. One who was very rich and a kingpin had escaped. It was told that he had been hiding in the house of a V.V.I.P. The detention orders passed by the Deputy Commissioner under M.I.S.A. were not confirmed by Government and they had lapsed after the due date. The Home Secretary to Government had questioned the propriety of the detention orders passed by the Deputy Commissioner. The top Police had prevailed upon the Deputy Commissioner to withdraw the suspension orders passed against the P.S.I.

It is not known whether the suspension orders passed by the Deputy Commissioner against the P.S.I. was given effect to. There was pressure on the Government to transfer the Deputy Commissioner. The Deputy Commissioner did not withdraw the suspension orders, as he had the powers to do so. No proceedings seemed to have been taken against the offenders for having committed atrocities on the Harijans".

5. *Case study of Mr. Mariswamy*

Mr. Mariswamy is a senior IPS Officer of the rank of Deputy Inspector General of Police. He is also an activist which is a rare combination. He has expressed his views on the Police and judiciary.

The Problem

"Civil Rights accrue to a person by reason of abolition of untouchability by Article 17 of the Constitution of India. Therefore, they are intimately connected with the existence of untouchability. Untouchables in India lived on the periphery of society, were denied all manner of rights and suffered a number of disabilities. They were prevented from entering temples and offering worship. They were denied access to shops, restaurants and places of public entertainment. They were prohibited from practising any occupation other than their traditional occupations and kept away from wells, tanks and taps. They were prevented from using public conveyance and wearing jewellery and finery. They were denied admission to hospitals and educational institutions. They were compelled to do degrading labour and insulted on the ground to untouchability.

The protection of Civil Rights Act seeks to prevent the practice of untouchability and remove all these disabilities. The practice of untouchability and the enforcement of various disabilities are offences under the Act and the persons violating them are punished with imprisonment and fines. There are other consequences also. The land and licences the offenders might have procured from Government stand the danger of cancellation. Any grants from the Government are to be suspended. If any officer fails to investigate an offence under the Act, he could be prosecuted for abetment. Punitive fines could be imposed on offending groups. It is also enjoined that the State must actually ensure that the Civil Rights are availed by the affected people.

The Agencies

The Government seeks to achieve the objectives of this law through mainly three existing agencies-the Police, the Deputy Commissioner and Social Welfare Officers and the Courts. The Police are given the duty of preventing offences under the Act and whenever offences take place, investigating them, apprehending the offenders and prosecuting them.

The disabilities under which the untouchables suffered for centuries were woven round a system of denial of wealth and education to them. They were prevented for ages from educating themselves, possessing land and other means wealth, and using jewellery and finery. If their disabilities are to be removed decent livelihood has to be created for every one of them. Several schemes have been formulated and a number of Departments are involved in implementing them. They are coordinated by the Deputy Commissioner and the Social Welfare Officer at the District level.

The judiciary also has a very valuable role to play. The judicial conviction is what ultimately deters offenders committing offences and not the mere registration of cases of arrest of offenders. Quick disposal of cases is therefore, important. The judicial magistrate after conviction can also make an order suspending licences and permits of the offender. The Director of Social Welfare is the link between the Executive agencies at the district level and the State Government. He coordinates developmental activities designed to uplift the Scheduled Castes. The Civil Rights Enforcement Cell looks into cases of special importance that are committed against the Scheduled Castes.

Limitations

The Law relating to the Civil Rights is fairly elaborate. Besides religious and social disabilities it takes care of issues like social boycott and repriasals. Economic and social transformation is recognised to be necessary for the enjoyment of these rights and schemes have been formulated with the declared aim of improving their standard of life. These schemes and the law have not made any impact and the life of the untouchables has registered only a marginal improvement. It is in this context we have examined the limitations, self imposed or otherwise, of the implementing agencies.

Inefficient Administration

The administration in India is characterised by low morale, low efficiency and low performance. The Government employees are comparatively well paid and have securit y of tenure. They enjoy a better standard of living and have imbibed a feudalistic outlook. There is pervasive corruption. Manufacturing of Statistics to suit ones ends is common. There is no accountability. There are no incentives for good work and punishment for lapses. The common man's lot is miserable. If this is the case with regard to Government work in general, will it not be unnatural to expect it to be different in the case of this particular piece of legislation ? Further the Scheduled Castes people are economically and socially weaker than others. Their ability to get work done is minimal. Therefore, there is even wilful violation of the provisions of law. There are cases where the magistrates have failed to award minimum punishments. This applies to other areas also.

Over-Burdened Agencies

The agencies which are entrusted with this responsibility are already over-burdened with more pressing matters. The Police have to attend to crime and law and order problems besides having some responsibility for the enforcement of a number of Acts. The Deputy Commissioner is having a finger in every pie. Collection of land revenues, administration of developmental works and some responsibility or other in every kind of work in the District has left him with meetings and meetings. He has been incapable of doing any sustained work. The judiciary is also over-burdened. Cases keep mounting in the courts. Judicial delays have become legendary. Cases take years to come up. Thus the picture of administration is one of diffused responsibility and confused attitudes. As a result, unless a matter is of extreme importance it tends to get neglected.

Wrong Appreciation of Need

The Scheduled Castes problem differs from other problems in vital aspects. It is a problem which has social, economic and emotional over tones. To tackle these effectively and to remove the persons to an environment of self help and self respect, all round sustained assistances over a period of time is necessary. Today officers distribute cattle or fowls, attend to emergent problems and return home thinking that their work has been done. Some time back I happened to discuss this matter with a Deputy Commissioner and while he admitted that it is possible that the existing schemes are not self contained and not beneficial in the long run he shrugged his shoulders off and said the Government does what it can and it is for the beneficiaries to make use of it to their benefit. This is characteristic of the approach of these agencies to the problem. Unfortunately the social and economic dependence of the Scheduled Castes on others is so great that this kind of quick appearance and disappearance does not help. Unless continued assistance is provided to these persons they are likely to suffer and come more under the obligation of their exploitors".

CHAPTER VI

Conclusions and Recommendations

The study on 'Evaluation of the Effectiveness of Protection of Civil Rights Act, 1955' has two unique features, namely (1) it is first of its kind in the country even though Section 15-A of the Act clearly envisages periodical surveys. Secondly, this study is not generally in the nature of comprehensive academic research. The broad objeciives and main questions have been briefly mentioned in the Introductory Chapter. The various difficulties and limitations have also been mentioned.

It is in this context that an attempt is made to draw certain broad conclusions and suggest suitable recommendations which are not exhaustive, but only illustrative. The broad conclusions are:

Awareness

The study reveals that in general there is a very low level of awareness of the various legislations among the people, both victims and oppressors. The fact that only around one-fourth of the respondents have known the existence of Law is a sad reflection on the administration. The position would have been still worse but for the inclusion of Kerala.

When analysed with reference to the extent of knowledge of Law, the situation becomes still more alarming.

Awareness of the latest legal position is also generally wanting among the Law enforcement authorities. Police generally stands exposed. Two decades since the PCR Act came into existence are not adequate to educate the people about legal provisions. Law has a social mission. Its success would very much depend upon the awareness and responses of the people. It is here, according to the findings of study that the State has miserably failed. Neither the people to whom it is made, nor the people against whom it is made are generally aware of the very Law. And finally the very administrative machinery that has to enforce the Law is also familiar with all the important provisions of Law.

Further the study reveals that it is only during the last five years that there is a take-off in understanding about the existence of the Law.

Certain major and significant measures like special courts, mobile courts, summary trial, collective fine, cognizable offence, broader coverage of the area of untouchability are generally not known to the people. In fact. special and mobile courts either do not exist at all or are limited and even where established, they are not functioning effectively. This is what is learnt from the study.

The measures of the State to impart thorough and updated legal knowledge are generally questionable. Regular and sincere efforts have not been initiated by State. Conferences, seminars, group discussions etc., are generally lacking.

CRE Cell

One of the major findings and reinforcement of general criticisms is related to the Civil Rights Enforcement Cell/Police squads. A number of deficiencies inherent in this system have almost wrecked the very structure. It has become more of a laughing stock than a helpful agency.

The study shows that it has neither adequate number of officers nor enough powers. There is no uniformity among the four Southern States. There is no coordinating body. If in one State an officer of the rank of an Inspector General of Police heads the Cell/Squad, in some other States only officers of the rank of Superintendents of Police are in charge.

The number of hands to assist is also meagre. The Cell has to depend upon the regular police force. It has no powers to investigate and proceed further. It is a parasite depending upon the Police in the various districts.

It cannot function independently. Excess of interference of the higher ups and politicians is not ruled out. Its reports are either half-truths or are uncared for. The Government issues instructions not to proceed against those who have produced false caste certificates and got into Government jobs. The Cell is expected to look into the non-implementation of reservations and economic deprivations. But in practice, the Cell rarely takes up or is allowed to take up faithfully.

The Cell has to depend upon the Public Prosecutors for the trial in courts. These prosecutors are the employees of State Government and are controlled by the Director of Public Prosecution. The Cell cannot wag its tail. It is rather the tail that wags the Cell.

Another feature of the Cell is that it often provides shelter to those Police Officers who are not in the good books of the higher officers or politicians. Sometimes those who desire transfer to metropolitan cities are accommodated. Further, it is seen that these officers are frequently transferred, creating big gaps in the system. This affects the smooth and effective functioning of the cell.

Maintenance of updated and well planned and designed documents relating to PCR cases, might from the stage of registration of complaints till the date of disposal by the Courts is a basic requirement. But the study reveals that the records are generally poorly maintained. Updated statistical information is not readily available. There is utter confusion in the statistical particulars furnished.

Cases registered during each year the cases brought forward from the previous years are often combined and the particulars on cases ending in conviction, acquittal and pending are conflicting. Cases pending with Police and the court are not generally separated. It means in brief no attempts have been made to maintain and provide systematic data.

Role of Police

Police comes under heavy attack. Scheduled Caste respondents have lost faith in the present culture of the Police system. The fact that there is delay coupled with attempts to refuse to register cases brought by the victims would mean that the Police is generally not interested in ensuring safety of the Scheduled Castes and imlementation of the PCR Act.

Another important conclusion is that the Police force is totally inadequate and almost incompetent to raise to the occasion. It is admitted that the fate of the victims would depend solely on the Police and the judiciary. But the argument in favour of judiciary that it has to depend upon forces beyond its reach seems to be valid to a large extent. Police has to build the records, prepare the witnesses and create confidence among the weaker sections. But the present study indicates, in no uncertain words that the Police has generally failed.

The Police has no right to resort to compromises between the victims and oppressors. Yet Police does it. This would mean that the Police wants to protect the oppressors when they are wrong and punish the Scheduled Castes if found wrong. This double standard behaviour of the Police is a clear reflection of the caste politics. It is evident from the reactions of the Scheduled Caste repondents that non-Brahmin upper caste Hindu Police officers are generally not helpful to the Scheduled Castes.

Yet another distressing fact is that the Police, though not always and everywhere, are in the habit of changing the nature of the offence committed. In between punishment under IPC and PCR cases, punishment is more severe under the PCR Act. The Police for obvious reasons brings the cases under the provisions of IPC. It implies that where the Police has no option but to initiate suitable action, it tends to act under the IPC. This would again mean that the Police is not objective and duty-bound.

Another revealing feature of the analysis is that the Scheduled Castes repose more confidençe among the minority religious group of Police officers than their own caste officers. The argument that if the Scheduled Caste Police officers take bold steps strictly according to Law, they are criticised for favouring Scheduled Castes seems to be valid. While generally the caste-Hindu Police officers other than the Brahmins are known for their apathy, the Scheduled Caste officers are known for slow and cautious approach for fear of bias, the minority group Police officers are in better position to deal with the situation and provide relief to the Scheduled Castes as required under the PCR Act.

Social Pressure

Social pressure is well recognised and admitted. Our social system is such that at times one has to yieled to pressure. The study reveals that the Police often comes under pressure either from the politicians or their superior officers. This would also mean that even honest and upright officers also come under pressure some times.

This was particularly so that level of the Constables and Sub-Inspectors. These officers yield to pressure because of lack of support to them later on. It means our administrative system is vulnerable and does not provide protection to law-abiding and enforcing Policemen.

Another dimension of this social pressure tactics is that though judiciary is not helpful to the victims, nowhere was it mentioned that the judges come under pressure and their judgement is based on this. It is true that there is a strong criticism against the judicial system, but certainly not against the judges.

Consequences

It is also seen that the Scheduled Castes do not lodge complaints with the Police so easily because of the consequences. The caste-Hindus not only harass them and practice social distance, but also do not tolerate complaints being lodged against them. Three major consequences are : threats issued by the caste Hindus ; grudge of the caste-Hindus and atrocities. This would imply that some safeguards should be extended to the Scheduled Castes to enable them to lodge complaints with the Police.

Role of Judiciary

That the judiciary is a very slow moving institution is well known. There may be several reasons, justifiable or unjustifiable for this. The public image of our judicial system is very poor, though often judges may not be solely responsible for this damage. What is more relevant and distressing is the fact that cases under the PCR Act are treated very badly. The fact that hardly 2% cases are decided in favour of the victims is unbelievable, but yet it is a reality. Who can respose faith in this system ?

This distress gets reinforced when the acquittal and pending issues are probed into. The conclusion that could safely be drawn is that acquittal is the rule, whereas conviction is an exception. Pendency is still worse. This would imply that the existing judicial system is not favourable to the Scheduled Castes in general and the victims in particular. In other words, the legal system extends a safe protection to the people who violate legal prescriptions and destroy human dignity and rights.

The new law does not permit compounding of cases under any circumstances when once brought to the Court. But in reality, it was not so till 1986. The fact that there were some cases which were compounded by the Courts would expose the ignorance of Law by the judges. It means again that the keepers of Law do not keep themselves abrest of latest legal position. This again warrants some remedial measures.

Witnesses

Another important conclusion is that it is some times difficult to obtain witnesses for fear of the caste-Hindus, loss of jobs and income. The present incentives to obtain the witnesses are inadequate. To sustain the witnesses till the end of the case, some realistic approach is needed. Legal aid scheme is not popular among the Scheduled Castes.

Connected with the problem of the witnesses is the problem of having useful Police force. It emerges from the study that the Police is ineffective. Besides this, Police is under pressure and not adequately trained. This makes out a case for creating a new kind of Police force that stands for neutrality and commited to duty.

Visits

One of the miserable failures of the administration is the fact that the official circulars that the Police and Revenue officers should visit the Harijan areas for enthusing confidence in them and educating them are observed more in their breach than implementation. It is seen from the study that though the visits are occasional by and large, sincerity in purpose is generally lacking. The purpose for which they have to visits and report is generally defeated. It all depends upon the personal attributes of the officers.

What is further implied from this social situation is that monitoring and evaluation attempts are either not contemplated or neglected.

Committees

Though the Act envisages setting up of committees to supervise the working of the Act and suggest necessary measures for improvement, the study shows the negative trend on the part of the State. The types of committees, the way in which they function, their accountability and responsibility are not at all satisfactory. Committess exist on paper. No definite records of proceedings, follow-up action are generally maintained.

Peace Committees

One of the measures of the State is establishment of Peace Committees. The usefulness of this is questioned by majority of the activists. It implies that the Peace committees serve no purpose in the present form. Setting up of Peace committees on adhoo basis is unlikely to help ease social tensions and conflicts.

False Complaints

There is a general notion that the Scheduled Castes take undue advantage of certain legal measures and take revenge against the caste-Hindus by filing false complaints. But the study rejects this theory by and large. The fact that 61% Non-Scheduled Caste respondents say that the complaints are real should summarily dismiss any such feelings against the Scheduled Castes.

Role of Activists

The increased role of the Activists has definitely resulted in increased cases under PCR Act coming to surface. There is a conflicting claim over the increased number of cases reported. Is it because of the better role of the Police or because of the better role of the Activists. The study lends support to the fact that the emergence of organizations like Dalit Sangharsh Samities and the comitted role of the leaders have definitely led to increased cases brought to the Police Station. This is not to rule out the due share to the administration, whatever be its drawbacks in the given social realities.

Futurity

Based on the findings of the study, it can also be concluded that the future is further complicated. There is going to be better awareness among the Scheduled Castes due to inter-play of various forces and the resistance of the Caste Hindus to the challenges. This results in more and more conflicts, murders, rapes and so on. To avoid this, the State should contemplate measures right now, both punitive and corrective as well as short range and long range policies and measures.

Though several decades are over since the Constitutional ban on the practice of untouchability and several legal and administrative measures have been undertaken by the State, it is seen from the present study that social discrimination is still practised in many areas of social interactions like entry into temple, religious processions, hotels and other areas of social discrimination.

At the same time, the present study points that there is some definite change in all these areas compared to the past. Efforts to eliminate the practice of social distance have definitely borne fruits. The future is not bleak. Hopes could be raised that with better efforts in all directions, the social situation can still be improved.

Inter-State Variations

Since the study has to throw some light on inter-State comparative position, some conclusions need to be mentioned in this regard. The PCR Act has impact on the people of Kerala to a very large extent. Understanding of the legal position, role of the officers, courts, awareness of the measures of the State are better in Kerala when compared to the other States. This position of Kerala is due to various factors such as peoples educational background, social mobility among the people, influence of communism and Sri Narayana Guru, a great Saint and social reformer.

Next comes Tamil Nadu which has witnessed the strong movement for self-respect and equality launched by the late E.V. Ramaswamy Naiker or Periyar. The Backward class movement has had its own effect in this State.

Karnataka comes third. The situation still calls for better efforts. The heinous crimes committed in Bendegere where Scheduled Caste youths were forced to consume human excreta and the accused were finally let off by the Court have shaken the confidence of the Scheduled Castes. Dalit Sangharsh Samiti is actively engaged in educating the Scheduled Castes to raise their arms against social discrimination and exploitation.

Andhra Pradesh with its worst feudal lords deriving strength from caste and class is the fourth among the Southern States. Almost in every area probed into, it provides a disappointing and painful situation.

Though the PCR Act is common to all these States, there are sharp differences among them in matters relating to the CRE Cell, special and mobile courts and other related issues. Though Karnataka, Andhra Pradesh and Tamil Nadu have set up special courts they suffer from lack of adequacy and poor performance.

In none of these States, there is any single instance of 'collective fine' having been imposed so far. Further, not even a single survey has been undertaken as required under Section 15-A of the Act. The other measures envisaged under this Section are also either marginally fulfilled or not at all implemented.

In short, excepting Kerala, all the remaining States have failed to a larger extent in effective implementation of the PCR Act.

Recommendations

Based on the field experience coupled with the general discussions held with knowledgeable persons, certain broad recommendations are offered to enable the State force effective implementation of the provisions of the Protection of Civil Rights Act.

1. *CRE Cell*

The Civil Rights Enforcement Cell should be made an autonomous body with all powers under the Commission of Enquiry Act. It should not be subjected to the controls of the State Executive. It should be directly under the control of the National Commission for Scheduled Castes and Scheduled Tribes or the Ministry of Home Affairs, Government of India.

There should be uniformity in structure and functions of the Cell. The present Police squads and Civil Rights Cells in some States should be re-designated as Civil Rights Enforcement Cell.

The CRE Cell should be headed by an Inspector General of Police. At the State Headquarters, where the Cell is located, there should be one Superintendent of Police and two Deputy Superintendents of Police. Adequate office and executive staff should be provided.

There is a need to have a research unit consisting of one trained Sociologist and one Economist along with necessary subordinate staff. This unit should probe into the social situation and maintain all relevant documents with latest statistical information.

A well designed proforma has to be supplied to all the States. This proforma should give a comprehensive picture of the situation. A model proforma is also suggested. It is the statutory responsibitity of all concerned to furnish uptodate and reliable information of the Cell through the Proforma. Each district unit should have this information available at any time. The Central Cell should collect this information and have a consolidated statement.

Any case not registered or registered but not chargesheeted should have an explanation and have the approval of the higher officers. A separate document should be maintained for this purpose. Similarly, conversion of PCR cases to IPC cases should also have the approval of the CRE cell and this should be documented and available for inspection.

Any lapse on the part of the Police while registering and charge-sheeting should be viewed seriously and deterrant punishment should be given. Similarly, good work done should be appreciated and rewarded. In fact, a systematic follow-up of the behaviour of the Police while dealing with the cases and the Scheduled Castes should be documented and this should be taken into account for awarding merit certificates, promotions etc.

At the district level, the Additional Superintendent of Police should be placed in charge of the PCR cases and he should be responsible, responsive and accountable to the Director of CRE cell. He should have necessary secretarial assistance. A clear linkage between him and the Police officers at different taluk and village level should be established and should have functional relevance.

There seems to be a need for establishing divisional or zonal offices in each State with a Police officer of the rank of a Deputy Inspector General of Police. For economy purpose, the present D.I.Gs posted to various divisions may be designated for this purpose. They have to shoulder this responsibility besides their routine works.

Thus, a well designed hierarchical system of CRE Cell with

adequate staff, autonomous Status, powers, finance is inevitable if justice and human dignity needs to be preserved.

The CRE cell should have its own prosecutors with mobile jurisdiction. This measure is inevitable if justice has to be given fairly and quickly to the victims.

Further, CRE Cell should be headed and assisted by Police officers with rich experience, ability and commitment. As desired by the Scheduled Castes in general, it seems desirable to post offlcers from the minority and Backward caste groups to the extent possible. These officers should be given fairly attractive incentives and allowances.

The CRE cell has to monitor the implementation of reservation policy and take suitable action against the defaulters. All recruitment authorities including Universities, Statutory bodies, public undertakings and aided institutions should be covered.

Similarly, false caste certificate question should be seriously dealt with by the Cell. It should not allow the Government to protect the culprits under any circumstances. Relevant steps should be taken up to device ways and means of issuing caste-certificates, not allowing any scope for mischief or manipulations.

The Cell has to do a lot to ensure that the land-grant policy of the State is not defeated. Attempts to deprive the Scheduled Castes of the benefit of grant of land should be curbed. This is a great task ahead of the Cell.

2. Coordinating Body

At the Central Government level, there should be a body to coordinate with all the CRE Cells in the various States. As said earlier, this coordinating cell could be attached to the National Commission for Scheduled Castes and Scheduled Tribes or to the Home Department of Government of India.

There should be frequent meetings, conferences and Workshops involving all the CRE Cells, Scheduled Caste activists,

Police, judiciary and voluntary organizations involved in Scheduled Caste and Scheduled Tribe problems.

Similarly, there should be intensive educational programmes to effect certain amount of attitudinal changes among the caste-Hindus. Several measures to promote social integration and harmony need to be contemplated. Religious leaders could also be involved in this movement.

3. Special/Mobile Courts

Special courts and mobile courts can be combined into one category, namely special mobils courts as done in Andhra Pradesh. These courts should move to the area where the offence has been committed in order to solve the various problems of obtaining witnesses, time consumption and economic loss. Summary trial is inevitable. Simple but reliable procedures should be adopted.

Another problem is the tendency to prefer appeals to the higher courts where justice may be denied to the Scheduled Caste victims. All the efforts made to secure prompt and fair justice at the lower level may be defeated. Hence, appeals should be filed before a specially constituted judicial body called 'Civil Rights Appellate Authority'. This body should again consist of committed and fair minded judges. There should be no more scope for appeals.

4. Training

In order to ensure proper and timely action by the officers and judges, it is also desirable to arrange training courses, workshops and study groups among them. Police training colleges and schools should have regular and frequent classes conducted and at the end of the training/workshop, tests should be conducted to assess their understanding of the legal and administrative measures.

Similarly, judges, particularly at the lower level, should also be exposed to refresher courses at regular intervals. Retired judges of the rank of District Judge may be in-charge of running these courses. This is only to avoid the possible reluctance or hesitation on the part of the judges under the supervision of administrative officers.

5. *Visits*

Designated officers should be made to visits the villages, meet the Harijans in their areas, listen to them, create confidence in them and be-friend them. Similarly, they should also visits the areas of the caste-Hindus and educate them. The ultimate goal should be to promote good relationship between the two groups and eliminate social taboos and discriminations.

Regular records should be maintained by the officers. These records should be inspected by the higher officers who should also visits the areas randomly and record their opinion. Voluntary organizations and interested individuals should be allowed to go through these records.

6. *Village Institutions*

Another measure of long range significance is to locate as many as possible institutions in the Scheduled Caste areas. Cooperative societies, Balwadies, schools, Mahila Mandals, Youth Associations training and workshops, drinking water facilities etc. could be located in Scheduled Caste areas. Caste-Hindus may have initial hesitation. But in course of time, they will get adjusted.

7. *Solidarity Committees*

Social solidarity committees should be established in all the villages or at least in the disturbed areas on permanent basis. These committees should have such members who are knowledgeable, and who command respect and confidence. Government should assist these committees to arrange meetings and cultural activities. Religious leaders should also address the people.

8. Meetings

The long range corrective measures should be well planned and executed. Social harmony cannot be established in a highly fragmented and disturbed society. The process is definitely slow since attitudes are based on deeply rooted prejudices and misconceptions.

Frequent meetings should be held in the villages. Local youths of different caste groups should be identified and motivated to take up the responsibitity of social integration. Youth festivals, Youth clubs etc., should be promoted. Mahila Mandals consisting of women of all groups should be actively involved. Similarly children should be encouraged to mix freely both in the school premises and outside. Children's clubs should be encouraged.

Legal literacy programmes should be made an integral part of the overall adult education policy. Printed literature in the local language explaining in brief the legal provisions and the need for a strong, united society could be emphasised. For the bencfit of illiterates, non-formal methods are to be adopted.

School teachers and youths to be motivated to take the lead. Good work should be recognized and rewarded.

9. Incentives

In order to enable the victims and the witnesses to give evidence before the Court, greater incentives need to be paid to them. This should cover enhanced and attractive travel allowances as well as daily allowances. The loss of income should be adequately made up.

It is also desirable to ensure prompt recovery of collective fine from the whole village community subject to the provisions of the Act. Collective fine should be adequate to meet all these expenses and should also be a lesson to the people.

10. Panchayat Raj

Panchayati Raj Institutions have to play greater realistic role.

There is no use in having statutory provisions without being put into practice. The SC/ST Welfare Committees should have realistic programmes and adequate finances. Besides reservation of seats for SC/ST on Panchayat bodies, it is also desirable to reserve the offices of Presidents/Chairman of these bodies in a suitable and practicable manner. This change in the management of village political institutions will enthuse confidence among the Scheduled Castes and at the same time it will dilute the traditional controls of the caste-Hindus.

11. Survey

Periodical surveys by independent agencies be conducted at a regular interval of every five years. Research projects should be cleared without any fuss. Surveys should be done in each State. Combined States will pose field work problems. A comparative analysis can be done later when individual State reports are made available.

In order to ensure common features in the survey/research reports, meaningful interview-schedules and questionnaires be designed and given to all the concerned Project Directors. Limited freedom can be given to the research team to meet the special requirements.

Proforma I.

Relating to PCR Cases
(for the use of the Police)

State :
Date

Year	*No. of cases brought to the Station*	*No. of cases registered under different nature of offence*	*No. of cases rejected under different nature of offence*	*Reasons of rejecting*
1	2	3	4	5

Whether approval of the higher officers taken for rejection	*No. of cases charge-sheeted*	*No. of cases pending investigation-Specify period*	*No. of cases converted from PCR to IPC*	*Reasons for this*
6	7	8	9	10

Proforma II.

State :

Date :

Relating to PCR Cases
(for the use of the Court)

Year	*No. of cases pending as on 1st Jan. of the year*	*No. of fresh cases filed before the year*	*No. of cases disposed off during the year*	*No. of cases ending in conviction*
1	2	3	4	5

No. of cases ending acquittal	*Reasons for acquittal*	*Cases pending trail-with No. of years*	*No. of cases compounded*
6	7	8	9

Reasons for compounding	*No. of years generally taken for disposal*	*No. of times cases adjourned*	*Reasons for adjournment*	*Remarks*
10	11	12	13	14

Index